LISTENING IN

LISTENING IN

A Multicultural Reading of the Psalms

Stephen Breck Reid

ABINGDON PRESS
Nashville

Library of Congress Cataloging-in-Publication Data

Reid, Stephen Breck.
  Listening in : a multicultural reading of the Psalms / Stephen Breck Reid
    p. cm.
  Includes bibliographical refernces.
  ISBN 0-687-01194-9 (alk. paper)
    1. Bible. O.T. Psalms—Criticism, interpretation, etc.
  2. Multiculturalism—Religious aspects—Christianity.
  3. Minorities—United States—Religious life.   I. Title.
  BS1430.2.R43   1997
  223'.206—dc21   97-42691
                                                                  CIP

97 98 99 00 01 02 03 04 05 06— 10 9 8 7 6 5 4 3 2 1

MANUFACTURED IN THE UNITED STATES OF AMERICA

CONTENTS

CHAPTER 1

The Conflictual Self

Once a bird began to fly south to hibernate. The bird tired and fell to the ground amidst a deep snow drift. A kindly cow picked the bird up with her tail and plopped the bird in a heap of warm cow dung. Just about the time the bird felt warm and refreshed, a paw picked the bird out of the dung heap. The paw belonged to a wolf. Moral: Not everyone who puts you in a pile of dung is your enemy and not everyone who rescues you from a pile of dung is your friend.

People! How long shall my honor suffer shame?
Psalm 4:3; Eng 2

All my enemies shall be ashamed and sorely troubled.
They shall turn back and be put to shame in a moment.
Psalm 6:11; Eng 10

The world of antiquity presents us with material that indicates more than one set of listening contexts or contexts for concern. One context speaks of personal conflict as an expression of lay piety. The psalms of lay piety reflect mostly circumstances of sickness and persecution in which an antagonist designates the psalmist as "other" and "enemy." The other listening context speaks to the corporate royal and cultic concerns as an expression of official religion, a context in which the maintenance of the institution of the royal household and the temple dominate.

Because the self lives in a world of conflict which is complex and visceral, it becomes an existential reality and theological resource for a hermeneutics of suspicion. The designation "enemy" provides a way of speaking about that conflict. The morality tales that are part of American economic and political life point to just such a world of conflict. One of these morality tales is the myth of the mob at the gate.

During World War II the Japanese became America's enemies; following the war that role was filled by the Soviets. Both were our "mob at the gate."[1] The politics of conflict feeds on the mob at the gate story. At times the story construes the mob as those outside our borders. However, sometimes the story portrays the mob, not as those at a distance but rather as those closer to home who differ by race, class, or gender.

One day, while we were living in Berkeley, our tree fell down, and we called someone to remove it. When I spoke on the phone to the individual who came to take care of the tree, I discovered that he had a Ph.D. in church history. He told me that because of affirmative action there were no jobs in church history for white men. He would be employed if it were not for the mob of women and people of color at the gate of academic institutions. At a denominational meeting a young man complained that he could have been one of the preachers at the conference, but they had to have women and people of color. He, too, had his professional aspirations cut short by that mob at the gate of preacher selection. Other examples abound, but allow these to suffice to indicate the contours of the myth of the mob at the gate.

Blues and Laments: Conflict as Theological Resource

> The Blues is an impulse to keep the painful details and episodes of a brutal experience alive in one's aching consciousness, to finger its jagged grain and to transcend it . . . by squeezing from it a near-tragic, near-comic lyricism.
>
> Ralph Ellison

Laments have certain characteristics, one of which is tenacity. When Christmas has been over for weeks, we know how tenacious tinsel is. It is still on the floor and the door mat where we took the naked tree after the season was over. But the tinsel reminds one not of the joy that is Christmas but rather the sadness of the season. Many people did not get the Christmas spirit. A dark gloomy depression that is as tenacious as the tinsel without the tree enshrouds many people during the holiday season. In the same way the blues/laments enshroud and cling to us, refusing to let go.

When Billie Holiday sings "Good Morning Heartache," or when the tattered tinsel is around, we should take time with our heartache; the laments charge us to do that. Often we rush too quickly to the good news and the happy times. Rather we should follow Billie Holiday's point—a point echoed by the laments—"Good morning heart ache, sit down."

What Makes a Lament?

Three subjects dominate the laments in the Psalter: God, the one who laments, and the enemy. Individual laments often contain negative petitions such as *do not be silent* (Ps 109:1; 28:1; 39:12) or *do not hide* (Pss 27:9; 55:1; 69:17; 102:2; 143:7).[2] The plot of the lament typically includes the reality of the psalmist's alienation, conflict with another person(s), and sense of the absence of the responsive God.

Westermann points out that laments do not function as the end of a process. Rather, in a lament the congregation moves from plea to praise. The lament uses a narrative tension which finds resolution in a song of thanksgiving. As such, the lament ends in unrestrained praise.

Brueggemann explains this movement from plea to praise as the revolutionary element in laments. "The lament form thus concerns the redistribution of power."[3] If one subverts the lament and swiftly moves to praise, the lament is lost with disastrous consequences. Then one must stand at the door recovering the used tinsel of grief, the energy of the lament.

Recovery of the Laments

When one rushes through a lament to find happiness, the genuine covenant interaction is lost. One of my seminary professors was in the midst of a series of small disasters. In talking with his wife, he shared his anger with God in this situation. His wife said to him, "You can't feel that way about God!" He responded, "I am sure that God is big enough to handle my anger." Anger and loss are a necessary part of intimacy, genuine covenant, and interaction. Without them a relationship remains superficial. Recall the melodious tones of

Nancy Wilson as she reminds us, "You don't know what love is until you've learned the meaning of the blues." Without heartbreak (or lament) we are without love, intimacy and covenant.

Laments begin with the realization that something is not right. The psychologist John Bradshaw has proposed that anger is nature's way of telling us something is wrong. Laments begin with just such a feeling. In Psalm 6:2–6 (Eng 1–5) the psalmist calls God to account for the present situation and petitions God to rectify it.

There are two individual lament forms. The first describes the experience of being falsely accused; the second describes the experience of illness. Both of these focus on the interplay of alienation and community. Falsely accused people become marginalized in society. The ill become similarly marginalized because their illness stands as a mark of their sin.

Not all laments come in an individual form. But we should notice that even the communal laments describe the experience of alienation and relationship (see Pss 60, 74, 83). The image of the silent God and the cacophony of the enemies recurs in the laments (see Pss 22:2–3, Eng 1–2; 28:1; 31:18, Eng 17; 35:22–24; 50:3, 16–21; 83:2, Eng 1; and 94:16–17). When you study the laments in the comfort of your home and church, take time with your own heartache and the heartaches of those in your family and neighborhood. Tinsel is tenacious, but our God is even more so.

LISTENING IN TO THE PSALMS

The first-person speech we find in individual laments is almost always human speech and tends to fall into three categories. First are the "I" statements which reflect vulnerability, innocence, and trust; second, are the statements of loyalty; and third, we encounter performative (liturgical) language, such as "I will give thanks."

Conflict in the Laments

Both implicit and explicit conflict are found in the laments. Explicit psalms encompass primarily interaction with enemies while the implicit psalms narrate the psalmist's dialogue with inner demons.

Adversarial Psalms

A number of psalms describe explicit conflict. The terms used most often to describe this adversarial relationship are the enemies (*'oybîm*) and the wicked (*rĕ'šāîm*). "Even in purely private enmities, projection plays a significant role, as in the case in which someone is my enemy because I am hostile toward him (subjective) and not only because he is hostile toward me (objective)."[4] A part of the conflict in the blues is its visceral quality, no matter how submerged.

The language of wickedness, enemies, and shame bespeaks a rhetorical situation in which a perceived ethical dualism seems appropriate speech. This ethical dualism in the psalms lays the foundation for the ethical dualism of later Jewish apocalyptic. The problem becomes whether this belies some Jewish conflict that we do not clearly know.[5]

The identity of the adversaries has occupied much of the debate about the explicit conflict described in the personal laments. Ultimately the search for the identity of the adversaries has yielded limited results. Generally, the references are of rather generic conflict. This preoccupation with the identity of the adversaries has resulted in deflecting a grasp of the tone in the laments and the conflictual nature of human existence. Croft's position is that the enemies present a threat to the psalmist, and the wicked exhibit an infuriating unawareness of the psalmist's plight. This position presents an interesting scenario, but one that does not find support in the material. Sheppard's position that the enemies are those in the prayer meeting with the psalmist is most intriguing, but definitive evidence seems to be lacking.

However, the interpretive issue at stake is not the identity of the adversaries *per se*. If the writer wanted us to know the identity of the enemies, a clearer path would have been presented. No, the interpretive key is the "that-ness" (that there is an adversary) not the "who-ness" (the identity of said enemy).

Enemies

The enemies (*'oybîm*) usually describe those who pose a threat. The reaction to the psalmist by an antagonist determines the designation. Generally the sins of the enemies determine their reaction to the suppliant's condition.

Psalm 3

The use of rhetorical questions (such as "how many?") is a device the psalmist will use again and again in the laments. In the second part of the line, the psalmist answers the question *how many?* with the phrase *many*.

In verse 2 (Eng 1), we find the term for opponents (*sārāy*) which stands in parallel to those who *rise against me* (*qāmîm*). The language of "rise" has spatial and sociological implications. The psalmist has a lower social status and is described by the enemies as being theologically isolated. The psalmist puts words into the mouths of these opponents: *There is no help for you in God* (NRSV, 3:2). God's relationship to the psalmist and to the conflict are themes which recur a number of times in the laments.

Following the speech of the enemies, the psalmist witnesses to a reliance on God followed by four "I" statements. *I will cry out my voice* (3:5; Eng 4). This first "I" statement elicits God's response. Responsiveness by God empowers the voice of the psalmist. Without God's response the psalmist's voice lacks a resonating ear and falls lifeless to the ground. God's responsiveness is located on the mountain of God's holiness. God's responsiveness now has both a geographical as well as a political context, Zion.

The second and third "I" statements accent the theme of trust and assurance. *I lie down and sleep* and *I wake again* (3:6; Eng 5). These statements declare that God sustains (*samak*) the ongoing activity of the psalmist.

The final "I" statement uses the negative in order to emphasize the sense of trust. The psalmist does not fear his enemies, and there are over ten thousand. Opponents have surrounded the psalmist, but they generate no fear.

Now the psalmist has established a relationship with God through the statement of God's responsiveness, so the psalmist can move to the plea, *Arise, O LORD, and deliver me my God* (3:8; Eng 7). Earlier the psalmist used the verb "rise" with relation to the opponents (3:2; Eng 1b); now a form of the same verb "arise" is used to describe a reversal brought about by God (3:8; Eng 7).

"I" statements of the psalmist are replaced in the last section by "You" statements about God. *For you strike all my enemies on the cheek; break the teeth of the wicked* (NRSV, 3:7). Here the psalmist brings in two new terms for the opponents: enemies (*'oybîm*) and the wicked (*rě'šāîm*). There is no reason to think of any of these opponents as outside the believing community. From this psalm we cannot discern any difference between the adversaries.

The psalm ends with a benediction. *Deliverance belongs to the LORD; may your blessing be on your people!* (3:9; Eng 8). Even though this is an individual lament, the end is corporate.

Notice the voice and answering on the one hand and the conflict on the other. The conflictual self of the Psalter presupposes a conversation between the psalmist and God. This "I-Thou" dialogue depicts a vocal and present person speaking with a responsive God.

Psalm 13

Here, once again, the psalm begins with a call for help. Notice how the psalmist uses the question how long? four times. The verbs that accompany these questions: forget (*shakah*); hide (*satar*); and bear pain (*'asab*) are verbs of absence as contrasted to the verb used in connection with the enemies which forms the last question (13:2–3; Eng 1–2). The psalmist cries in distress while God elevates the psalmist's enemies.

We find the term "how long?" (*'ad 'anah* four times in this short psalm. "Despite its brevity, Psalm 13 is unique in the psalter in beginning with an extremely forceful plea to Yahweh to intervene. . . ."[6] The plea provides a refrain *how long?* in verses 2–3 (Eng 1–2) which points to "the prolonged nature of the distress."[7]

Images of the elusive nature of God in time of crisis are noted in the first verse by the verbs "forget" (*shakah*) and "hide" (*satar*). These are verbs of absence, and the other side of the absence of God is the growing invisibility of the believer.

The images of absence in this refrain give way, quite naturally, to descriptions of distress. There is a contrast between the *grief in the heart all day* and *the enemy now exalted* (13:3; Eng 2). The former recounts absence and the latter distress.

A turning point occurs in the psalm in verse 4 (Eng 3a) as it shifts to verbs of presence. The psalmist directs God to look, consider (*nabat*) and answer (*'anah*). The psalmist argues that the failure of God to intervene will lead to the loss of integrity in God's justice by assuming that loyalty protects one from the enemy. In order to make this point, the psalmist uses the imperative and verbs of response and relationship.

The psalm ends with a reaffirmation of the psalmist's loyalty to God. *Yet I have trusted in your solidarity; my heart rejoices in your salvation. I will sing to the* Lord *because God has dealt bountifully with me* (13:6–7; Eng 5–6).

Psalm 30

In Psalm 30, the psalmist speaks from the edge of the abyss, an abyss which takes many forms. One form the abyss takes in our lives is "but." Sometimes we will meet someone who is dead because of "but." This person can still walk and talk, but he/she is dead because their feelings, joys, and hopes have been killed. Some of us have been in the Pit/Sheol created by "but" ("I would *but*. . . ." or "It could have been *but*. . . ."). The psalmist proclaims a freedom from "but."

This song of thanksgiving recounts the movement from the fringe of life and death as the psalm begins with a traditional formula. *I will lift you up,* Lord (30:2; Eng 1b). The verbs give an interesting pattern in their formula, in which the psalmist lifts up God.

A *kî* clause conveys the reason for praise. The *kî* clause is typically an adverbial clause introduced by a conjunction indicating relationship between the independent clause and the dependent clause in terms of time, cause or reason, purpose or result, or condition. The verbs focus on God's redemptive action on behalf of the psalmist: drawn, healed, lifted up, and restored. These verbs dominate the first section (30:2–4; Eng 1–3),[8] telling us that the psalmist has been lifted up as God might draw a bucket from a well. The well contains the water that brings life, but that same water can also drown. The religious institutional presence and health is a matter of God's honor and hence should receive God's franchise, i.e. church growth at divine behest. Likewise the psalmist notes that the vindication and status of the psalmist reflects well on God, thereby growing God's supporters. God's redemptive activity plays into the social conflict as the psalmist tells us and thanks God that the enemies did not obtain gladness at the psalmist's expense. The success of the illness would have carried with it the implicit victory of the psalmist's enemies.

In the second section, there is a contrast between God's faithfulness and the wavering of the psalmist (30:6–8; Eng 5–7). The introduction, which invites the hearer to join in the celebration—*Sing praises, righteous ones of God, and give thanks to the remembrance of God's holiness* (30:5; Eng 4)—demonstrates a communal faith even though this is a personal psalm.

Moving from a *kî* clause describing the action of God in the first section, the second section builds on the nature of God. God's anger lasts but a moment; *God's favor lasts a lifetime. In the evening weeping abides, but in the morning joy* (30:6; Eng 5). This power captures us, but then the psalmist applies this contrast to the human experience: *I say in the midst of my prosperity, 'I shall not be moved forever.' LORD in your favor you caused me to stand as a strong mountain; you hid your face. I was terrified* (30:7–8; Eng 6–7). A moment away from God produces terror despite the proud claims we make in the comfort of our lives.

The next section (30:9–11; Eng 8–10) continues with the tone of vulnerability and moves into a lament and plea with God. Similar to other psalms, we hear the psalmist trying to persuade God that maintenance of the psalmist presents a "church growth" possibility.

The final section describes again God's redemptive activity. *You turned mourning to dancing, opened my sackcloth, girded me in gladness. For that reason my honor sings to you and could not keep silent. The LORD is my God. I will give thanks to you forever* (30:12–13; Eng 11–12).

The superscription at the very beginning tells us something about how this personal psalm came to us through the phalanx of editors and priests. This superscription connecting the text and *Hanukkah*, a service commemorating the rededication of the temple, makes the point that the death recounted in the psalm represents both a personal and a communal experience.

Psalm 31

The first two "I" statements in this psalm describe a sense of fragility and dependence. *In you, O LORD, I seek refuge; do not ever let me be put to shame* (31:2; Eng 1) parallels the later verse, repeated in the New Testament, *Into your hand I commit my spirit; you have redeemed me* (31:6; Eng 5). The themes of fragility and dependence come through clearly in this psalm by way of the references to shame and the list of several types of adversaries.

The next two "I" statements connect ideas of trust and worship. *I trust (batah) in the LORD. I will shout exultingly and rejoice in your solidarity* (31:7b-8a; Eng 6b-7a). This trust is contrasted to those who keep idols (31:7a; Eng 6a). The foundation for the "I" statements is found in the "You" statements introduced with the term *ašer*, here translated "because" (31:8b; Eng 7b). God's sight and knowledge of the psalmist's affliction propels the next two "You" statements as well as the "I" statements that precede. *You have not delivered me into the hand of the enemy ('oyēb). You have caused my feet to stand in a broad place* (31:9; Eng 8).

The next "I" statement brings the reader back to the sense of distress and fragility on the one hand, and the plea to God on the other. *Be gracious to me, O LORD, for I am in distress* (31:10a; Eng 9a). The psalmist explains the distress with a series of qualifiers:

> *My eye wastes away in vexation,*
> *my soul and body as well.*
> *For my life is spent with sorrow,*
> *and my years with sighing;*
> *my strength fails*
> *because of my iniquity,*
> *and my bones waste away* (31:10b-11; Eng 9b-10).

"I" statements of vulnerability continue. The psalmist recounts isolation, humiliation and slander (31:12–14; Eng 11–13).

Then the tone shifts as the psalmist returns to a psalm of trust (31:15–25; Eng 14–24). *I trust in you, LORD, I say, "You are my God"* (31:15; Eng 14). With the trust comes a plea which is broken down into two parts, deliverance and vindication. *Deliver me from the hands of my enemies and from my pursuers* (31:16b; Eng 15b). The social dimension of deliverance means vindication and the absence of shame. Therefore, the psalmist continues the plea. *LORD, do not let me be put to shame for I call upon you. Let the wicked (rĕʿšāîm) be put to shame* (31:18; Eng 17). The wicked present the model of a generic adversary, but we do not get any specifics about their crimes.

The final "I" statements indicate a military context for the conflict. *Blessed be the LORD for God has done a wonderful thing. God's solidarity is with me in times of trouble. And I said in my trepidation, "I am cut off from in front of your eyes. But surely you heard my voice of supplication when I cried out to you* (31:22–23; Eng 21–22). A new theme is introduced here in which deliverance comes even in the midst of the apparent absence of God. The theme of the apparent absence of God plays a large role in other laments, such as Psalm 22.

The conclusion of the psalm conveys the final tone in a theme of trust. Even amidst the apparent absence of God, trust prevails. Hence the conclusion: *Be strong and let your hearts take courage, all you who wait for the LORD* (31:25; Eng 24).

Psalm 102

Even the superscription labels this as a personal lament (102:1 Heb; the superscription is not given a verse number in English). *LORD, hear my prayer, and my cry goes to you. Do not hide your face from me on the day of my distress. Incline your ear to me. On the day I cry out, quickly answer me* (102:2–3; Eng 1–2).

The "I" statements accent the situation of the psalmist by comparing it to a solitary bird.

> *I forget to eat my bread.*
> *Because of my loud groaning, my bones cling to my skin.*
> *I am like an owl of the wilderness,*
> *like an owl of the waste places.*
> *I lie awake, and I am like a lonely bird on a housetop*
> (102:5b-8; Eng 4b-7).

"My enemies" are described as persistent persecutors (102:9a; Eng 8a). In this regard they resemble the enemies in Psalms 69 and 71.

The sickly circumstance of the psalmist contrast with the robust position of God. *You, LORD, are enthroned forever, indeed the remembrance of you is from generation to generation* (102:13; Eng 12). God's position is enhanced not only by power but by longevity (102:26–29; Eng 25–28).

Psalm 143

Psalm 143 is found in Book Four of the Psalter. Because this section typically contains hymns of praise, finding a personal lament here seems strange. However, when we notice the nature of the "I" statements in this psalm, we have an idea why it fits its present context.

Like many of the personal laments, it begins with a call to hear. Also like a number of the laments we have examined, we find a request for God's answer. *Hear my prayer, O LORD; give ear to my supplications* (requests for favor/mercy; *taḥănûn*). *In your faithfulness, answer me in your righteousness* (143:1).

The "I" statements in this psalm are consistently words of trust. *I remember the days of old. I think about all your deeds. I muse on the work of your hands. I stretch out my hands to you* (143:5–6). This psalm also returns to the theme of the apparent absence of God. *Answer me quickly, O LORD; my spirit fails. Do not hide your face from me* (143:7a). This time the psalmist describes the responsiveness of God as something one can hear. *Let me hear in the morning your solidarity because I trusted in you* (143:8a).

One has to wonder about the relationship of "teach me" (143:8b) and "save me" (143:9a). *The enemy pursues my soul* (143:3a) describes the active persecution often connected with the term "enemy." When the psalmist talks about salvation from "my enemy" in verse 9, the salvation referred to seems to be concerned with epistemological more than military or even sociological salvation. But, nonetheless, God will exterminate all the opponents of the psalmist's soul. The loyalty the psalmist expresses toward God prompts a superior loyalty from God—a loyalty that means the enemies of the psalmist must succumb to the judgment of God.

Psalm 55

Psalm 55 is one of the most poignant psalms of lament. While other psalms have drawn a picture of the isolation of the psalmist, here the psalmist describes an intimate betrayal (55:13–15; Eng 12–14).

The superscription does not give a clue to the affective context of the psalm, merely a reference to the musical and liturgical setting. The psalm then moves into a call to hear what we have noticed in a number of laments. *God incline your ear to my prayer* (55:2; Eng 1). The call to hear attaches itself to an expression of the absence of God. The absence of God comes through as a lack of God's attentiveness. Both the negative and positive statements in the verse make the same request to "be present" in the conversation.

Then the psalm moves into "I" statements. This group of "I" statements, like other laments, includes statements of vulnerability. *I am troubled . . . I am distraught* (55:3b; Eng 2b). The adversaries are both the enemies and the wicked (55:4; Eng 3). In this case both of these adversaries are equally active against the psalmist.

In an earlier psalm, the psalmist uses the language of the solitary owl as a metaphor for the suffering believer. In Psalm 55 the psalmist gleans another metaphor from the world of birds for the sufferer's experience. This time, however, the psalmist uses the dove to capture the sense of vulnerability and freedom. *And I say, "O that I had wings like a dove! I would fly away and be at rest"* (55:7; Eng 6). This statement was transformed by the black hymn writer Albert E. Brumley in his hymn "I'll Fly Away."[9]

The violence which the psalmist perceives occasions the retaliation of God (55:10; Eng 9). We should probably point out that this psalm refers to what seems to be economic crimes. In other laments the crimes tend to be character assassinations, although even these had economic consequences.

In Psalm 55 the enemy is close to the psalmist. *It is not an enemy who taunts me. . . . It is not one who hates me who assumes great airs. I could hide from that one. But it is you* (55:13–14; Eng 12–13). The false friend, the false "you," must be dealt with, so the psalmist moves to the first person plea. *I will call upon God. . . . I will complain and I will murmur* (55:17a, 18; Eng 16a, 17). The pleas provoke God's response. *The* LORD *will save me* (55:17b; Eng 16b) and *will hear my voice* (55:18b; Eng 17b). The false "you" (human) of verse 14 (Eng 13) contrasts with the true

"You" (divine) in other verses. Hence, the psalmist concludes with a statement of loyalty to the true "You" (55:24; Eng 23).

The psalms of lament remind us that the human situation will constantly present us with crisis and conflict. Amidst this circumstance the psalmist instructs the reader to trust in the true "You." Even in the midst of the apparent absence of God, the issue of trust in the one reliable "You" continues.

Wicked

The term "wicked" (*rĕšāîm*) usually describes those who pose no physical threat to the psalmist. They are defined by their location in God's judgment, not by matters of race or nationality, and are often identified with the wealthy.

Psalm 12

Psalm 12 describes the predatory nature of the wicked. The psalm begins like many laments with a theme of vulnerability. *Help, O LORD, for there is no longer anyone who is loyal, for the faithful have disappeared from humankind* (12:2; Eng 1).

The "I" statements in this psalm are not in the mouth of the psalmist. Rather the psalmist seems to be quoting a divine edict prompted by the adversity of the believing community. The wicked prowl round about, and God's protection thwarts them (12:9; Eng 8). The Hebrew verb *hālak* (walk) here is translated "prowl" because of the term "round about" (*sābîb*). "To walk" is itself a neutral term, but "to walk around in a surrounding fashion" takes on a more ominous tone. Hence, the translation "prowl" seems an appropriate description of the wicked's activities.

Psalm 26

Vindicate me, LORD, for I walk in my innocence, and in the LORD I trust (26:1). "Walk" refers to the social intercourse of the psalmist. The subsequent "I" statements continue as testimonies of innocence. *I walk in your faithfulness* (26:3). These "I" statements seem reminiscent of the description of the righteous in Psalm 1. *I do not sit with the worthless, nor do I consort with hypocrites; I hate the company of evildoers, and will not sit with the wicked. I wash my hands in innocence* (NRSV, 26:4–6). The psalmist does not describe the activity of the wicked;

rather the psalmist merely draws a word picture of a world with competing communities. The important point for the psalmist is *I walk in my integrity* (26:11a).[10]

Psalm 28

Psalm 28 also begins with a call to hear. *To you, O LORD, I call; My Rock, do not be silent before me* (28:1). The call to hear stands as a request for protection from the absence of God as represented by God's unresponsiveness.

The psalmist makes it clear what is at stake. *I will resemble those who go down to the Pit* (28:1c). This prompts the psalmist to continue a plea with an "I" statement. *As I cry out for help to you, as I lift up my hands to your holy sanctuary* (28:2).

The psalmist wants to avoid the fate of the wicked who are described as the disingenuous (28:3). Do the white folk in Richard Wright's novel, *Native Son*[11], represent the wicked? They are people who often interact with black folk and have no sense of themselves. Their duplicity eludes even their own self-consciousness.

Psalsm 141

This Psalm of David begins with a typical opening. *LORD, I call to you. Come quickly to me. Give ear to my voice when I call upon you* (141:1). God and the psalmist have a relationship designed as a responsive one. The voice of the psalmist is a link between him and God, and God pays attention to this link.

The psalmist does draw an explicit picture of the wicked in that they set traps for the psalmist. Their fate should be that they fall into their own traps. *Let the wicked fall into their own nets while I alone escape* (NRSV, 141:10). The term for the foes comes from the verb, *sārar*, which means "to cause distress." Sometimes the word for foes refers to those who cause the distress (see Pss 10:5; 60:13–14; Eng 11–12; and 78:42). Sometimes we find it in synonymous relationship to the term "enemy" (See Pss 31:9, 12; Eng 8, 11; 42:10–11; Eng 9–10; 69:19–20; Eng 18–19).

Prayers of Persecution

Illness is but one of the expressions of social conflict and loss of esteem. This conflict displays itself more plainly in the psalms of persecution. Four elements appear repeatedly: a fervent cry, descriptions of threat and persecution, cursing of the enemies, and declaration of public praise of God.[12]

Psalm 64

For several years I began my course in Hebrew Bible with a collection of movie clips that, in my opinion, exemplified the realities of ministry. One of the clips came from the opening of the movie *Silverado*. It begins with a man sleeping in an isolated cabin. Suddenly shots ring out from several undisclosed spots, and he responds. Persecution strikes us from ambush like the man asleep in the cabin. In order to grasp the prayers of persecution, we notice the depiction of ambush in Psalm 64.

Three issues come to the fore in this psalm: first, the psalmist presents us with the anxiety of human conflict; second, the psalmist challenges us to ponder the perplexity of this conflict;[13] and third, the psalmist makes the point that the antagonists find their punishment in the tools of their trade, mean speech.

Listen to the psalmist's opening petition. *Hear, God, my voice* (64:2a; Eng 1a). Once again the psalm begins with a cry for divine intervention. This prayer is prompted by more than the persecution described in the body of the psalm. Social conflict in a closed society, like ancient Israel, generates the by-product of isolation. The call for God to hear moves the psalmist from isolation to reconciliation with God.

Again the psalmist must reckon with an enemy. An accumulation of descriptions of adversaries accents the conflict. As anxiety comes through in the psalmist's words, note the role of speech and esteem in this psalm. The adversaries are involved in character assassination; therefore, they have tongues like swords and words like arrows (64:4; Eng 3).

The psalmist asks God for a hiding place. The hiding place given by God contrasts with the hiding places used by the enemies as they wait in ambush to shoot like the faceless men in the movie *Silverado*. The language of ambush and the description of the reckless and covert nature of the attack (64:5; Eng 4) indicate the illicit nature of the conflict. The ambushers can afford to be reckless, if they have the protection of good cover.

When the metaphor used to describe the attack on the psalmist becomes the metaphor for divine retribution, the tone changes (64:8; Eng 7). Arrows that can wound the innocent can likewise be turned to injure the guilty. The psalmist brings out the irony that the weapons of the adversaries can ruin them. "What goes around, comes around."

Finally, the psalm closes with a short statement of trust (64:11; Eng 10) and with the exhortation to praise God in public. The persecution happens in public; therefore, the reconciliation must happen in public. The psalm began with the call to hear and the psalm ends with a call to rejoice in God's hearing. Both the conflict and the praise find their proper context in the public arena.

Psalms of Sickness

In antiquity illness represented more than the presence of disease. It was a metaphor to demonstrate divine disfavor. Social contact and esteem were connected with sickness and wellness in antiquity. On closer inspection, this should not strike us as unusual. In her book *Illness as Metaphor* Susan Sontag reminds us that illness fulfills a similar role in modernity as well.[14] Illness functioned as a context for shame in antiquity. When we blame the sick one, is it to make of that person an enemy? The psalmist often describes falsely accused persons who are also ill (see Pss 13; 22; 31:10–25; Eng 9–24; and 102).

Psalm 6

The seven penitential psalms, often recited on Ash Wednesday, begin with Psalm 6 (along with Pss 32, 38, 51, 102, 130, and 143). Even though Psalm 6 is liturgically understood as a penitential psalm, the main issue for the psalmist is marginality.

The psalm depends on a relational premise, namely the power of God and the unworthy status of the psalmist. When the psalmist begs LORD, *do not reprove me in your anger, or discipline me in your rage* (6:2; Eng 1), the lament moves from a relational premise. This first petition includes the negative imperative, *do not!*

The psalmist does not request freedom from reproof or discipline, but rather asks that the LORD exercise such reproof out of something other than anger and rage. All relationships experience ruptures requiring reproof and reconciliation; however, we hope that others will reprove and discipline us from their generosity. Hence, in the petition *Be gracious to me, LORD* (6:3a; Eng 2a) we see the language of vulnerability. Contrary to the negative imperative in the earlier section, now we find a positive imperative. In order to give the petition for grace a context, the psalmist shares a first-hand account of vulnerability signaled by a *kî* (result) clause, *because I am feeble* (6:3a; Eng 2a). In order to draw attention to the emphasis in the petition, the psalmist uses the emphatic personal pronoun "I."

Once the witness to vulnerability has occurred, the psalmist returns to requests, this time an entreaty for divine healing. *Heal me, LORD, for disturbed are my bones; my soul is greatly disturbed* (6:3b-4a; Eng 2b-3a). Repeating the pattern of a petition followed by a statement of vulnerability, this section moves out of the assumption that God answers all the psalmist's petitions. In other words, God is responsive. It concludes with a question to the responsive God. *But You, LORD—Until when ('ad mātāy)?* (6:4b; Eng 3b)

Our next petition likewise conveys a positive imperative using the language of vulnerability in order to elicit God's response. *Repent, O LORD; rescue my soul; save me for the sake of your loyalty/solidarity* (6:5; Eng 4). Indicated here are dual story lines or plots of human vulnerability and divine responsiveness. Only the psalmist's rescue and salvation will demonstrate God's turning. Not only does the psalmist define the content of divine repentance, but the psalmist also goes on to give rationale for this intervention. The Hebrew word *lĕma'an* (for the sake of) introduces the rationale for God's deliverance of the psalmist in the future. The psalmist continues *because there is no remembrance of you in death (and furthermore) who can give thanks to you in Sheol* (6:5c-6; Eng 4c-5). The human tasks consist of remembrance and thanks to God, but death subverts the human vocation of the believer.

The psalmist then returns us to the reality of the distress which overcomes him and his endurance. *I grow weary with my moaning. I swim* (in my tears) *all night* (every night) *on my bed. With my tears my couch I drench* (6:7; Eng 6). The distress, depicted as tears, overcomes the psalmist so much that tears provide a pool to swim in on the couch.

Verse 7 provides a transition while continuing the theme of overcoming distress. *My eye wastes away from grief/anger; it grows weak from all my foes* (6:8; Eng 7). The foes cause distress, and weakness of the eye is a metaphor used in the Hebrew Bible to indicate old age and nearness to death.

The final section (6:9–11; Eng 8–10) displays a confidence beginning with a warning to the workers of evil. The rationale for the warning presents itself clearly in that the responsiveness of God spells disaster for workers of evil. *Depart from me all workers of iniquity because the LORD has heard the sound of my weeping. The LORD has heard my petitions. The LORD my prayer accepts. Ashamed and greatly troubled shall be all my enemies. They shall turn around ashamed in a moment.*

The fate of the enemies is formulaic in this psalm because we do not have any description of the enemies who are the source of the psalmist's problems. More than a judicial character, the shame and trouble of the enemies functions as proof of God's responsiveness to the psalmist. At the same time, this psalm reminds the modern reader of the reality of conflict, although the conflict is not described here. Instead the psalmist assumes a conflictual world, where enemies exist and persist.

The repetition of the term *shema* (hear) gives witness to the reality that grounds the psalmist's world. The conflictual world of human life has a broader context given to it by a God who can hear the sound of our weeping.

Psalm 35

The "I" statement *I am your salvation* (35:3b) introduces a series of curses. The conflict is with those who pursue, but the references to the enemies (v. 19) do not have any clear indication that they are outside of the community. The most extensive use of the first person occurs in verses 11 to 18. The "I" statements function as statements of indictment and innocence. The psalmist claims that his past solidarity with the sick is a symbol of righteousness. The section ends with an "I" statement which is also a vow concerning worship.

However, worship in this case verifies issues of social location as well as an act of praise. The psalmist's access to the great congregation and the mighty throng demonstrates his reconciliation with the broader community.

Again the psalm raises the theme of the apparent absence of God. *How long will you look on?* (35:17). The psalmist continues with this theme in the final section. *You have seen, O LORD, do not be silent! O LORD, do not be distant from me! Wake up, arouse yourself* (35:22–23a). This "do not be distant" theme occurs also in Psalm 22. The language of honor and shame, coupled with the issues of labeling in this psalm, prevails in the psalms of sickness.

Psalm 41

Psalm 41, a wisdom psalm, concludes the first book of the Psalter (Pss 2–41). The psalm instructs the reader to compassion (41:2–4; Eng 1–3), models the plea of the distressed (5–10; Eng 4–9), and assures the listener of the presence of God (41:11–14; Eng 10–13).

Like Psalms 1 and 32, Psalm 41 begins with a blessing, "happy" ('*ašrê*). *Happy is the one who acts with insight concerning the poor* begins the psalm. The word used here for "poor" is *dal*. Acting with insight delineates the importance of relational, as opposed to disembodied, truth. God's delivery of the weak in the land (41:2–4; Eng 1–3) indicates that those who have treated the weak with generosity will also receive generosity and happiness.

We must address two interpretive questions before proceeding. Who are the poor? How do we act with insight? We will begin with the last question.

There was once a kind landlady who had one tenant. The tenant had a dog. He often failed to pay his rent on time. He also failed to buy food for the dog on a regular basis. Often she bought Elvis, the dog, the necessary food. One month he surprised his landlady by paying the rent only a week late. He also gave her some money for the dog food. He said he knew that she had been buying it. The landlady replied that she felt sorry for the hungry dog. He replied that he had read in the *Holistic Dog Book* that dogs don't need to eat every day. The landlady's response was lightning fast. She said, "I never read that book." Who of these two acted with insight concerning the dog?

The second question presents itself consistently in the debate over public policy. Who are the poor? The term "poor" (*dal*) occurs infrequently. The debate about its meaning will not be solved here; however, it does seem that this psalm refers to a small farmer living on the brink of insolvency. The psalmist takes the concern for right conduct toward God and augments it with right conduct toward the poor.[15]

The proverb (41:2; Eng 1) leads into a song of trust (41:3–4; Eng 2–3) which repeats the theme of blessing, *that one will be called happy,* as well as returning to a theme typical of individual laments, namely the protection from enemies. Protect a good name. Blessing has the connotation of esteem in this passage.

Then the psalmist describes injuries at the hands of his enemies (41:6–11; Eng 5–10) who are wishing he was dead. Even the attempts at care fall short; those who make a visit of hospitality only bring empty words. The psalmist describes his increasing isolation; even the peaceful friend (NRSV: "bosom friend") turns on the psalmist. A call for God's grace is repeated (41:11; Eng 10). The presence of God provides the focal point for a short song of trust followed by a benediction (41:12–13; Eng 11–12).

Psalm 86

The collection of Korahite psalms is broken up by Psalm 86, a psalm of protection. We find the typical petitions *Incline your ear* and *Preserve my life* (86:1–2). Embedded in the opening plea we find a statement of hope which involves the faith statement *You are my God* (86:2b; Eng 3b).

The psalmist describes himself as poor and needy, but we have no way of determining the social location and import of these categories. It could be that this is a way of talking about marginalization. It seems unlikely that we could, from these terms, ascertain anything about the comparative wealth of the psalmist.

Four common elements distinguish this believer's blues and laments: fervent cry for help; description of being persecuted or threatened by others; cursing of the enemies; and the praise of God before the congregation, a feature not found in the psalms of sickness. These psalms retain their place in the Psalter because they recount the blues of the disenfranchised believer. "The psalms we have preserved appear to have survived more for their distinctiveness than their conformity to a particular form or style."[16]

Summary Observations

There is a paradox in the personal laments. The psalmist describes the "other" as enemy and adversary; however, the scene described by the psalmist points out that the broader community designates the psalmist as the enemy and adversary.

These psalms are the laments of the mob at the gate, both historically and existentially. These "others" designated as enemies give witness, in the psalms of personal lament, to the conflict they experience.

LISTENING IN AT THE FOOT OF THE CROSS

The Psalter describes the circumstance of the conflictual self as involved with adversaries and the interaction with adversaries which generates conflict. In the midst of the conflict the psalmist experiences the apparent absence of God. Nonetheless, the psalmist maintains trust in God, not glibly but in the form of an existential and eschatological wager. As we listen in at the foot of the cross, we must ask, "how does the experience of the cross inform our understanding of these affirmations?" The first source for such questions is the New Testament.

Adversaries in the New Testament

The New Testament depicts the Christian Self as a conflictual self. Jesus says, according to the Gospel of Mark, *All who are not for us are against us* (Mark 9:40). The New Testament describes a life of struggle for the early Christians; they were conflictual selves, persons in the context of conflict.

The Psalter often understands the world in terms of conflicts and dichotomies, the enemies and the righteous. However, the New Testament makes a different turn. For instance, a look at the concordance demonstrates that "enemy" occurs more often in the Psalter than in the entire New Testament. We note also that the New Testament makes two important transformations from the Psalter. First, the "other" in the Hebrew Bible, especially the Psalms, becomes the "enemy." In the New Testament the "enemy" becomes the "other" and the "sibling." And second, the New Testament brings us face to face with the enemy within.

The External Enemy

We hear the word from Jesus: *Love your enemy/ies* (Matt 5:44 and Luke 6:27, 35). Leviticus 19:17–18 instructs the listener about hospitality to neighbors and kin. However, Jesus radicalizes this notion of hospitality by suggesting that love for the kindred and neighbor should be extended to all. Now even the "other" and the "enemy" find the benefit of hospitality tradition in Hebrew religion and Judaism.

One should not view this as some heroic church-growth strategy. What is at stake for the Christian is participation in the Christian family (Matt 5:45). To treat the "enemy" as "other" and then as "sibling" is an intrinsic element of Christian identity. It is what we do; it is who we are. To confuse it with the heroic is to lapse into naive hubris.

The aberration of this text in the church has denied that there is conflict. "The most persistent error of modern educators and moralists is the assumption that our social difficulties are due to the failure of social sciences to keep pace with the physical sciences which have created our technological civilization."[17] The Christian temptation to deny conflict or describe it as "bad taste"[18] trivializes the Sermon on the Mount. In such a case, the radicalization of hospitality transforms itself into the easy moralism of "being nice." The moralism "be nice" does not stand in the face of the more powerful morality tale of the mob at the gate, for then the reader no longer has the Bible but rather biblical moralism.

In the New Testament the Christian self is a conflictual self who, nonetheless, lives life as though the "enemy" and the "other" is a "sibling" in Christ, that is to say, in the family of God.

The Internal Enemy

Paul reminds us that we were the enemies not reconciled to God (Rom 5:10). In fact, we often move in ways contrary to our Christian Self. *I do not understand my own actions. For I do not do what I want, but I do the very thing I hate* (NRSV, Rom 7:15). Hence not only were we enemies in the past, we continue to internalize that which is antagonistic to God's work for humanity.

We have already described the reality of conflict in human existence. However, Paul makes a point about the radicality of the conflict. It is not only intrinsic to our context, it is intrinsic to our personality. Walt Kelly was right when his character Pogo said "We have met the enemy, and he is us." So, rather than demonizing the enemy, we take seriously the conflict between the self and the enemy—who is often the enemy *within* the self. We note that our opponents represent, in Pauline apocalyptic fashion, principalities and powers (Eph 6:12).

The Christian identity in the Cross and resurrection occasionally gives way to the practicality of conventional wisdom. Sin and greed, which fuel sexism and racism, have an intellectual infrastructure which humans internalize like mother's milk. Does this mean that Christians are in "recovery" with regard to sin, greed, sexism, or racism? Yes, in the sense that we shall never know a time when we shall not be enemies to our God as well as children of our God until the return of Christ. No, in the sense that the model of "recovery" is too therapeutic. Even though recovery has one participate in the group, that group does not participate in the vocation of the reign of God. Recovery does not fight the infrastructure of sin and greed. Recovery does not address the principalities and powers of racism and sexism. Recovery is a makeshift ecclesiology.

LISTENING IN TO CONTEMPORARY CULTURE

Adversaries: External Enemies

The life of conflict and the external enemy also occur in literature. Rudolfo Anaya describes the conflict between the *curandera*, Ultima, and the *bruja*, Tenorio, in his novel *Bless Me Ultima*. This novel recounts the coming of age of a teenage boy, Antonio, in New Mexico. "Ultima was a *curandera*, a woman who knew the herbs and the remedies of the ancients, a miracle-worker who could heal the sick. . . . And because a curandera had this power she was misunderstood and often suspected."[19] Tenorio, the *bruja*, wielded power for the love of power. He used remedies and spells for ill. In Anaya's novel, as elsewhere in the fiction of people of color, the conflict of Ultima and Tenorio is between the disenfranchised, rather than across race.

Slave narratives, on the other hand, make clear a sense of conflict. The slave experience engenders a conflictual self in every black person. The mob at the gate knows conflict exists. If it did not exist, they would not be at the gate but rather at the dinner party everyone else seems to attend. The conflict generates a culture of resistance as an ex-slave recounts the issue of theft by slaves.

> Blacks claimed they learned their "stealing" or "taking" from the biggest rogue of all, the white master. Another ex-bondsman offers his theological, anthropological insight:
> All you hear now is 'bout de nigger stealing' from dese here po' white devils. De whole cause of stealin' an' crime is 'cause dey fo'ced the nigger to do hit in dem back days. . . . White folks certainly taught niggers to steal. If they had given them enough to eat dey wouldn' have no cause to steal.[20]

The novel *Beloved* also describes the conflictual self. The author, Toni Morrison, introduces us to an interesting collection of characters. Baby Suggs the grandmother, Sethe the mother, Denver her daughter, Howard and Buglar the runaway sons, Halle Suggs (possibly Sethe's husband), Paul Garner and Beloved. The characters move between "Sweet Home," not a sweet home but the location of slavery in the South, and the haunted house on Bluestone in the "free" North. The character Baby Suggs describes the enemy in the following way. "There is no bad luck in the world but white folks."[21]

The Internal Enemy

The internal enemy eats away at the soul of a person to such a degree that sometimes people commit self-murder. The styles of self murder differ. Morrison's novel provides a window into the issues of conflict. The title notes the experience of self-murder and marginalization. It comes from Romans 9:25: *I will call them 'my people' which were not my people, and her 'beloved' which was not beloved.* The Romans passage comes from Hosea 2:23 (Eng 2:25) in which God transforms the bastard children of Hosea from *Lō' 'ammî* (not my people) to *'Ammî* (my people).

The house at 124 Bluestone Road and slavery function as the external enemies in the story. Narrative tension builds as Beloved (the ghost of a dead baby now grown to adulthood) slowly moves into the house and displaces everything else in Sethe's life. Beloved and the house working in concert displaced Paul D., an acquaintance from "Sweet Home" who loved Sethe.

The external enemy and the enemy within intertwine. Morrison describes it as "spiteful," "loud," and finally "quiet."[22] The place we live acts on us. It becomes a friend or an enemy. Neither Anaya nor Morrison draw much attention to Euro-American characters in their respective novels. However, Morrison wants to make the point that not every "other" is an enemy. Morrison does make sure that the depiction of Euro-Americans includes Amy Denver, the young Euro-American girl after whom Sethe named her daughter Denver.[23]

Beloved represents the enemy within that has a life of its own. Every black family in America lives in a "124 Bluestone" and has ghosts to dispel. Recently in Virginia a black family went to a resort that recreated the eighteenth century. There they found a black man who played the role of a slave. The children were scandalized that they were reminded of the time of slavery, because slavery and the recollection of slavery continues to prompt black self-murder. Slavery lasted for over two hundred years. More than one hundred years have passed since the Civil War. The three hundred-year-old ghost persists.

Absence of God

The reality of conflict and enemies relates to the matter of the apparent absence of God. In a world where God is ever present, the enemies become a transient annoyance. However, for the psalmist they are more than that. The presence and threat of the enemies prompts the sense of the absence of God. The Cross is the place that the Christian meets the absence of God and the presence of the Trinity.

Literature also speaks to conflict and the absence of God. Sandra Cisneros, in her collection of short stories entitled *The House on Mango Street*, has a character muse on the reason for her aunt's paralysis. Her Aunt Lupe was a swimmer who injured her spine while diving one day. But the little girl asks why. "Maybe the sky did not look the day she fell down. Maybe God was busy."[24]

This absence of God also comes into play in a scene from the novel *Beloved*. The absence of God and the presence of the enemy go hand in hand as if insome perverse game. After Sethe had managed to escape slavery, the slave catchers came to take her and her children. The task of slave catching was delicate because the quarry had to be brought in alive. "Unlike a snake or a bear, a dead nigger could not be skinned for profit and was not worth his own dead weight in coin."[25]

The absence of God comes through as again as Elie Wiesel recounts a story from the Holocaust. Wiesel tells of the execution of a young boy in the death camp. Upon seeing the sight, the narrator asks the question,

> "Where is God now?"
> And I heard a voice within me answer him:
> Where is He? Here He is—He is hanging here on this gallows. . . .
> That night the soup tasted of corpses.[26]

Music

Neither Billie Holiday nor Fats Waller were known for political radicality in their music. Nonetheless, Billie Holiday wrote the lament concerning lynching called "Bitter Fruit," and Fats Waller wrote a complaint about racism, "Why am I so Black and Blue?" These two songs demonstrate the way two artists raise the question of why African Americans are labeled as the enemy. W. E. B. DuBois examined this phenomenon in his study on the "sorrow songs." The examples of Fats Waller and Billie Holliday illustrate that the power of the "sorrow songs" for African Americans who would not label themselves in any way activist. The process of being designated "other" so intrudes into the life of people of color in America that it bubbles up in music and the arts. Likewise the experience of being designated "other" percolates up into the words of the psalmist in these laments.

Conclusion

Remember the moral of the story with which this chapter began: not everyone who puts you in a pile of dung is your enemy, but not everyone who rescues you is your friend. Many would call themselves our friends by demagoguery. Those who tell the story of the mob at the gate often claim to be our friends exposing our enemies. The story has a home with those who pose as the ones who would rescue us from the pile of dung we are caught in.

The "mob at the gate" may have begun as a way to deal with foreigners, but in our contemporary context it has become a way to talk about matters of race and gender. Those who differ from us in terms of gender and race, the others, have become enemies.

Much of our talk about diversity misses this point. Often when we talk about diversity we assume that we are talking about diversity among friends. By labeling the "other" as "enemy," that person no longer falls into the purview of diversity. If we quickly and facilely turn the other into the enemy, then we make a context ripe for unproductive ethnic and gender strife.

The individual psalms alert us to the reality of conflict and difference. Further they discern that, in the midst of that conflict, loyalty to God remains essential for life. The justice of God, namely to punish the enemies, remains central and the issues of honor and shame play this out. Our task involves finding our voice somewhere between false innocence and irrational independence.

The New Testament picks up these issues and adds a concern for the temptation to label the other as the enemy. It also reminds us of the enemy within. However, if we pursue a strategy that demonizes our opponents and those who disagree with us, then we move contrary to the New Testament teaching. We are to love the enemy. Further, we know that the enemy is all of us, and in all of us. Sometimes, as with Sethe, the enemy is structural, and when we internalize it, it becomes our ghost.

When the church sings "Sometimes I feel like a motherless child," it is music wafting up from the mob at the gate. Those of us who sing at the gate find ourselves orphans in a land of our own birth, strangers to our own families. The crucible of the laments is to trust in God even in the face of the apparent absence of God and the presence of the enemies.

CHAPTER 2

The Authoritative Self

I know the LORD,
God'll make a way
I know God will
(from an African-American spiritual)

Book One of the Psalter contains two key elements for our discussion: a conflictual self who experiences the world with a sense of vulnerability toward and connection to a God who at times appears absent; and the agency of the believer authorized by God. By using "authority" language I hope to avoid the debate about the nature of power as being coercive or persuasive.

Disempowering Myths

Two myths dominate the issues of power and authority in the North American context of difference. These differences are centered around race. First, the myth of innocence maintains that no one has power or authority, especially not the "other." Second, the myth of rot at the top contends that leadership is corrupt, especially the leadership of the "other."

The Myth of Innocence

In the previous chapter we explored the myth of the "mob at the gate." When people of color appropriate this myth and label Euro-Americans as the "other," a possible byproduct can be the myth of innocence. In vernacular this is sometimes called "could'a, should'a, and would'a" talk. When a person of color falls into "could'a, should'a, and would'a," for example, "We could'a done better without the white folks" then the mob at the gate myth becomes denial of agency.

The Myth of Rot at the Top

Howard Baker tells a story about an early campaign when he was fresh out of the armed forces and campaigning for his father. It was the last day, in fact the last hour, of the campaign. The polls were ready to close when they saw an old man sitting on a park bench. They went over to the old gentleman. Howard Baker, Sr., introduced himself by saying, "I'm Howard Baker and I am running for Congress. I hope you will give me your vote." Without even looking up the old man replied, "Never vote; it only encourages them."

Destructive myths such as that of rot at the top have a tenacious and dangerous hold on the contemporary American mind. We encounter this myth in its early form in stories like the Arthur and Robin Hood legends, which each in its own way makes the oblique point that kings ultimately provide ineffectual leadership. The royal psalms provide a theological counter to this insidious undermining of any sort of leadership or agency.

"A readiness to suspect 'Rot at the top'—a conviction that our major institutions are prone to corruption and irresponsibility—is an enduring aspect of the American character."[1] Using the royal psalms as a lens, we will explore the problems with this morality tale. However, we should know that it affects more than the ways we construe our political leaders. "[T]he myth of the 'Rot at the Top' tends to cycle, alternating its indictment between the two major realms of authority: political power and economic power."[2]

The rot at the top myth's most pernicious use comes from the able mouths of demagogues who apply this myth to the leadership of any group designated "the other." These opinion makers depict people of color and feminists as lacking competent and ethical leadership. People of color easily internalize this myth which comfortably plays into the myth of innocence. "Pity poor us; we have no power, and we have no leaders."

A different picture is presented in the Psalter of organized power and the ideology of ancient Israel and Judah. We find in the Psalter an ideal of leadership in which reciprocity looms large. Kings take power, yet they also provide a service. In exchange for this service they receive wealth and power. What service do they provide? As leaders and heroes, they model piety and politics, and they define what it means to be a social person in a given culture.

The myths of innocence and rot at the top short-circuit a more appropriate examination of covenants of leadership and agency, replacing them with stereotypes. Royal psalms give us a criterion for our covenants with our leaders, as well as delineating the responsibilities leaders have.

Following Scripture we find not a depiction of powerful leaders but rather of leaders, both authorized and unauthorized, for whom God is the catalyst of agency. When the myth of innocence is applied to the other, it concludes that the other has no power and that the God of the other also has no power. When we apply the myth of the other to ourselves, internalizing it, we risk believing that we as believers are powerless, and projecting the theological corollary of the powerlessness of God.

Such a position ignores the laments. Opponents of the psalmist continually posited that God could not help the psalmist, but the psalmist just as continually rejected such a notion. There is no authoritative self unless one can say that our God has power, for God is the source of authority. Therefore, this chapter begins with an examination of the authority of God.

According to Scripture, to be effective any exercise of power must be authorized by the source of all agency, namely God. The central symbol of authority in the Christian church is the cross. A teacher of mine once said "Your cross is only as big as your understanding of sin is deep." In the Psalter the laments emphasize the depth of human sin and need. Voices we hear from Asian Americans, Hispanic Americans and African Americans make clear that the way they have suffered at the hands of others demonstrates the depth of human sin. Therefore, in these voices the power of God's enthronement and the cross of Jesus Christ loom large on the theological horizon.

LISTENING IN ON THE YHWH MLK PSALMS

Social Context

The *YHWH mlk* psalms orient and re-orient the believer in the midst of a conflictual world. "The characteristic phrase in the enthronement psalms proper—one which often appears in the introduction—is 'Yahweh has become King,' *Yahweh mālok* (93:1; 97:1; 96:10)."[3] This parallels the enthronement of an earthly monarch.

Sigmund Mowinckel electrified the debate on these psalms by pointing out that the Hebrew can be rendered "be king" or "becomes king." In fact, more contemporary scholars tend to render this term "the LORD reigns."[4] Five characteristics mark these psalms: concern for all the earth, all peoples or all nations; references to other gods (lesser gods); signs of exaltation and kingship; characteristic acts of Yahweh; and expressions of an attitude of prayer before the heavenly king.[5]

This reign of God moves beyond nationalism, as Mowinckel points out. "The victory of Yahweh is also a catastrophe for all the *other gods.*"[6] God becomes sovereign of the whole earth, not just Israel, but this victory requires struggle. Themes of struggle and victory sometimes explicitly and always implicitly indicate issues of judgment.

The judgment theme connects with the issue of election which we see in the narrative traditions about the creation of Israel. The goals of these psalms involve the exhortation to praise and the recounting of how God has been good to the elect in the past and will be good to them in the future. The psalmist construes us as the elect.

Nonetheless, we should not consider the *YHWH mlk* to be theological daydreaming.

> Everything contained in the enthronement psalms ... gives the strongest impression of belonging to the actual present. ... But it is noticeable that the poets never *describe* this enthronement as such; they merely refer to it in hymnal form as something real and well known and which the audience also can understand.[7]

A historical enthronement festival is suggested by Mowinckel. "That is to say, these psalms presuppose and, from their very nature have sprung from and belong to, a festival, which has, at least from one point of view, been celebrated as a festival of the enthronement of Yahweh."[8] Mowinckel said then what anthropologists such as Victor Turner and Clifford Geertz tell us today. "In the cultic festival, past, present and future are welded into one."[9] Christmas, Passover, Hanukkah, and Easter all provide cultic festivals that build community by rehearsing the past in order to inform the present and future. However, we find little definitive evidence for a *YHWH mlk* festival.

For Mowinckel the enthronement psalms and the ritual they reflect come from the pre-exilic era. He balks at any theory which would date this material as late as Deutero-Isaiah.[10] On the other hand, Hans-Joachim Kraus makes a number of connections with Second Isaiah material (Isaiah 52:7) which convince him of a later dating of the material.[11]

A pre-exilic context might be considered for at least one of these psalms (Ps 93). We find little evidence to the contrary for others (Pss 96–99). However, along with other issues, the location of these psalms in Book Four indicates a post-exilic literary and liturgical context.[12]

Since Mowinckel four alternative readings of the *YHWH mlk* psalms have been put forward:

They celebrate the enthronement of the Lord in the New Year's festival.

They do not celebrate the enthronement in this only hypothetical festival.

They celebrate the enthronement of the Lord in the post-exilic period.

They celebrate the Lord's kingship but not in the context of the Autumn festival.[13]

Our goal here does not involve blessing one theory or another with regard to the festival. Gunkel, Mowinckel, and Weiser continue as minority opinions. More confusion than clarity exists with regard to the social context of these psalms. What we learn from their discussions, however, must continue to remind us of the issues: they outline the plausibility of the combination of affirmation of the sovereignty of God and some appropriate ritual; and, each in its own way, they make the connection between this affirmation of God and the understanding of the government (king). To put it in crasser terms, the *YHWH mlk* materials describe the identity of God. They also implicitly push us in terms of our political understandings.

The material is found in Book Four of the Psalter, which probably reflects a post-exilic edition. Book Four responds to the theological questions raised in Books One through Three. The *YHWH mlk* psalms, as a collection, embody the theological perspective of Book Four and its response to the trauma of exile.

In light of its social and theological dislocation the community retained three key theological affirmations: the LORD was king long before the monarchy; the LORD reigns over all the universe; and the LORD's reign will have more implications in the future.[14]

As we focus on a group of *YHWH mlk* (enthronement) psalms (Pss 47, 93, 96, 97, 98, 99 and the early part of 95),[15] we notice that most of them come from a small canonical collection (Pss 93 and 95–99). The major exception, Psalm 47, appears in the collection of the psalms attributed to Korahite in Book Two of the Psalter, which we will discuss later.

Two themes dominate Psalms 93 and 95–99: the doctrine of God as creator and cosmic Lord above all other gods or idols; and the vocation of the human community in the cosmos. That vocation is praise. The *YHWH mlk* psalms weave these two themes together by intertwining the implementation of praise which is empowered through a relationship with the creator and cosmic Lord and the agency of the authoritative self.

Psalm 93

The LORD reigns, clothed in majesty; the LORD is clothed, girded with strength (93:1a). Unlike the laments, here we discover no superscription to provide a narrative of affective context for the hymn. Psalm 93 begins with the mark of an enthronement psalm, with the Hebrew phrase *Yahweh mālok* ("the LORD reigns"). Repetition is used to accent the majestic and powerful elements that accompany the reign of God. The verb translated here as "girded" uses a Hebrew verb form that is reflexive,[16] indicating that the subject acts on itself. The psalmist depicts God as self-authorizing, emphasizing that no other entity gives God strength, an assertion which contradicts the modern claim that "God has no hands but our hands."

The psalmist then describes God as agent. When the psalms say, *The world is firmly established; it will not be dislodged* (93:1c), the inference is that the world is established by the God who reigns. The psalmist uses synonymous parallelism with the repetition of the term "established" to make the point that the world provides a throne for God. The world finds security in the service it provides to God as throne, as noted through the parallelism in verse 2 (93:1c-2). The antiquity of the world provides compelling evidence for the psalmist of the reality of the reign of God.

The next section describes cosmic witness to the power of God. The psalmist uses flood imagery and water chaos as metaphors. The use of the term *nĕhārôt*, which describes streams in other places, reminds us of the flooding process of the Egyptian rivers and the rituals of enthronement that happened in that season. The psalmist uses the comparative "more" in order to demonstrate the superiority of God to other deities (93:4).

The psalm ends with a statement of assurance using the phrase "very sure" which comes from the Hebrew *'āman* ("to be firm"). There seems to be a connection between security and the holiness of God. The process of establishing validates the authority of God.

Psalm 95

Psalm 95 is not a *YHWH mlk* hymn in the strict sense. Rather it provides a liturgy of the superiority of God over other gods which invokes a call to obedience. The psalm proceeds through an almost chiastic structure. After an introduction and call to worship (95:1–2) the psalmist moves the reader through creation (95:3–5), history of redemption (95:6–7), history of sin (95:8–9), and finally destruction (95:10–11). The history of redemption parallels the history of sin; creation can lead to destruction.

The psalm has no superscription, but rather begins with a call to sing (first person plural performative language). A recurring theme of this psalm is joyful noise as a response to the goodness of God.

The superiority of the LORD over other gods provides the reason for our allegiance (95:3). We find a reference to the creation and cosmic dimensions of God, giving us a further reason for our allegiance (95:4–5). An antiphonal response moves from the creation as reason of praise (95:3–5) to the relationship we have with God as the rationale for praise. This reversal gives us a good example of chiasm, the rhetorical inversion of parallel structures: a (95:3–6), b (95:6–7), b^{-1} (95:8–9), a^{-1} (95:10–11). This section also returns us to the theme of worship. Here we have a clear indication of a worship setting for this psalm, probably in some regular ritual.

The final section of the psalm contains second and first person address with God as the speaker. We hear a reference to the disobedience by the people of God at Meribah (which means "contention") and Massah (Exod 17:1–7; Num 20:1–13). The last section transforms our understanding of the beginning of the psalm, *Come, let us sing to the LORD*. The joy of this song is God's announcement of judgment against the contentious ones in the community of faith. The song of joy is a song of justice and judgment.

Psalm 96

The Hebrew text does not have a superscription, but the Septuagint (LXX) superscription associates this psalm with the building of the Temple. The reading "when the house was built after the captivity" seems to validate a late dating. The psalm has five pieces: 96:1–3, summons; 96:4–5, affirmation; 96:6, further testimony; 96:7–9, description of vocation; and 96:10–13, eschatological conclusion.

Like the psalm which immediately precedes it, Psalm 96 begins with communal performative language. *Sing to the LORD a new song.* The psalm weaves together the vocation of the believer, namely witness, and the description of God.

The psalm continues with a summons to announce (*bāśar*) and recount (*sapar*). *Announce from day to day God's salvation. Recount God's glory among the nations, God's marvelous works among all the peoples.* The psalmist then provides the rationale for the witness by using two *kî* clauses. *For the LORD is great and greatly to be praised; the LORD is feared above all gods. For all the gods of the peoples are idols, indeed, the LORD made the heavens* (96:4–5). This rationale contains an affirmation of the superiority of the LORD over other gods. It concludes by basing this superiority in God's founding activity. Further, it introduces the new theme of idolatry, which emphasizes the importance of loyalty and occurs often in the *YHWH mlk* psalms.

The performative language continues with the next section (96:7–9) with the term *hābû*, which comes from the root *yāhab*. The closest parallels are found in Psalm 29:1,2; 1 Chronicles 16:28, 29; and Deuteronomy 32:3. The Chronicles reference is probably dependent on Psalm 96; therefore, we will ignore it for the time being. The parallel in Deuteronomy 32 introduces the song of Moses, a recital of salvation history. The most helpful parallel is Psalm 29.

The beginning of Psalm 29 differs in only a few points from Psalm 96. Instead of *Ascribe to the LORD O families of the peoples* (Ps 96:7), Psalm 29 says *Ascribe to the LORD, O sons of gods* (29:1). Psalm 96 moves out of the divine council, the implied setting for Psalm 29, and into the international arena. Further, Psalm 96 adds *bring an offering and come into God's courts* (96:8b) and *tremble before God all the earth* (96:9b). Both of these expansions seem to be the psalmist's way of further describing what it meant to *worship the LORD in holy splendor* (96:9a). Most importantly, the parallel in Psalm 29:1b-2 (Eng 1–2) indicates that ascribing goes hand in hand with worshiping. The LXX superscription locates Psalm 96 in the Temple worship section; verse 6 corroborates this. *Honor and majesty are before God; strength and beauty are in God's sanctuary* (96:6). God's reign authorizes the Temple. The psalms (96 and 29) find resonance not only in other worship psalms but also in the poetry of Isaiah 40–55. In 1 Chronicles 16, Psalm 96 is quoted in its entirety and placed between Psalms 105 and 106.[17] These psalms are set aside for the dedication of sacred space described in 1 Chronicles 16. The psalm concludes with performative language which instructs the human participants. Then the psalmist directs the plant and animal life as well to be inanimate objects in worship. *Say among the nations, "The LORD reigns! The world is firmly established; it shall not be moved; God will judge the peoples with equity"* (96:10). Once again, the cosmic founding of the world undergirds the legislative and judicial authority of the LORD.

Not only the human community but the whole cosmos—heavens, earth, seas, and fields—are also invited to participate in the vocation of praise. *Let the heavens be glad, and let the earth rejoice; let the sea roar and all that fills it; let the field exult, and everything in it* (96:11–12a). The last verse accents the coming reign of God. In fact, the Christmas hymn "Joy to the World" picks up on the theme of the coming reign of God pictured in Psalm 96.

Psalm 97

While the other *YHWH mlk* psalms described a superiority of the LORD to other gods, Psalm 97 seems to concentrate on conflict. It begins with affirmation and a summons to worship. *The LORD reigns! Let the earth rejoice; let the many coastlands be glad* (97:1). Then the text moves into the traditional theophany images of smoke and clouds (97:2–3) and a description of God's cosmic power (97:4–5).

However, theological superiority gives way to theological conflict. *All worshipers of images are put to shame, those who make their boast in worthless idols; all gods bow down before God* (NRSV 97:7). *Those who love the LORD hate evil. God cherishes the souls of God's faithful. God rescues them from the hand of the wicked* (97:10).

Verse 8 gives the first reference to Zion in this section of *YHWH mlk* psalms, although references to the house of God do occur earlier (Pss 93:5; 96:6, 8). The reign of God has expression in particularity, in this case Zion. In this verse we find legislative and judicial references made to the LORD (see also 93:5 and 96:10). Even though the psalms do not use the same word, they do share vocabulary indicative of some judicial concern.

Psalm 98

A song.
Sing to the LORD a new song concerning the marvelous deeds
God has accomplished.
God alone brought victory
through God's right hand
and God's holy arm.
The LORD made known God's victory.
to the eyes of the nation God reveals the righteousness of God.
God remembered God's loyalty and God's faithfulness to the
house of Israel.
And all the ends of the earth saw the victory of our God. (98:1–3)

How can this be a new song for us? We have grown up with this song. Well, the answer goes something like this: When I was in California, I received a call from the admissions office late one June afternoon. They wanted me to take time to talk to a prospective black student.

A handsome, well-dressed black man about my age came into my office. He said he had seen me at the Bible study at Allen Temple in Oakland. Beginning with what I thought was one of my trusted and safe opening questions to prospective students, I said, "What brings you to seminary?"

"Well, my dad died about a year ago."

"I'm sorry," I said.

"He drank all his life, an active alcoholic. I knew he would kill himself through drinking. In fact, I went to see him before we moved here ten years ago. We shared our last goodbye. Not literally, I saw him other times, but I pictured him dead ten years ago. So I buried him then. I called it tying up loose ends, preparing for his death. I cut him out of my life from that day forward as anything but a memory. He lived ten years as a zombie, a living dead, in terms of my relationship with him."

As I heard this story, my mind raced. I knew from pastoral care classes this was a case of anticipatory grief. But this time, knowing did not help. This was not the time to bring that up.

The man went on, "I knew he was killing himself, so I did not get involved with him any more. But that is not the worst of it. Over the last few years, not only have I buried my father, but I have shut down all my relationships. They are all going to end. Why get involved? I became emotionally distant to my wife and children."

"That sounds pretty lonely," I said, trying to say something helpful.

But he continued as people do when the dike that holds their awareness and feelings begins to spring a leak. The words flowed and after a while, it seemed they gushed like a wave. "No, that is not the worst of it. I knew that my relationship with my wife would end someday. We wouldn't be in love. I knew my children would grow up, and we would be estranged. We wouldn't care. The worst of it is that I buried God. Then I was alone absolutely, utterly alone. I kept going to church, to be with my wife and children, to keep my place in the community, but I was absolutely utterly alone. I am hoping seminary will help me get connected again."

"These are the times," I said to myself, "that I wish I had taken one more pastoral care class." I couldn't tell him a seminary is not a church, not a hospital for lost souls. This was not the time for the speech that says, "We serve the church as an academic institution, a graduate school." He would get that speech later.

This young man buried God alive. He transformed God into a clock maker who, now that creation has started, says "I'm done" while collapsing on the couch on that first Sunday afternoon to watch the football game.

The young man buried God along with all sense of joy in life. He could no longer make a joyful noise about anything. This young man buried God. He traded all hope in the present in exchange for something in the future—and then gave up on the future as well.

Even though it was not warm in Berkeley that time of year, I could feel the sweat roll down my back and side. What could I say to this young man? We sat in silence. What could I say?

Psalm 98 was not a new song for this young man; he had heard the song before. Nonetheless, it became a new song. Not new as we might think of the newest version of the laundry detergent that is continually reinventing itself. The psalm was not "new" in the advertising department's sense of a way of tricking us into buying the same old thing while paying more money for it.

Rather it was new in the sense of the Hebrew word *hādoš* which, while it can mean "new," has a verb form which means "renew." I would suggest that we might read the beginning of our psalm *Sing to the* LORD *a renewing song* (a refreshing song; 98:1). If the song brings this man back from the grave, if this modern-day Lazarus can be called by the voice of Christ out of the cave, the tomb, then this is a refreshing, renewing song indeed.

What makes it new is the content, namely the confession of the LORD.[18] The confession of the LORD says that "our God is a way maker." This psalm refutes the burial of God. Psalm 98 is a psalm of praise which accents the sovereignty of God.[19] When we forget that, we bury God.

Sometimes we get discouraged, and we search for pious isolation or disingenuous innocence. Pious isolation contends that there are problems bigger than we can handle. The world is so big, all we can hope for in our city is maybe just a beautiful neighborhood. Recently, I was talking with a friend at a local restaurant. We came to the conclusion that Los Angeles was just too big to be manageable. In the eighties many of us came to the conclusion that homelessness was just too big a problem. The political economist Robert Reich in his new book *Work of Nations* describes this pious isolation. He describes an America where folk hunker down in their own neighborhoods and people build for themselves a world isolated from the universe of problems that are just too big.[20]

Pious isolation has a friend, disingenuous innocence. Disingenuous innocence takes the Harry Truman saying, "The buck stops here," and changes it into a new saying, "The buck stops any place *but* here." Don't blame me, I just work here.

This is not Tillich's "dreaming innocence" but rather a cynical disingenuous innocence. The bigger problem comes from the corollary theology. When we say we have no power, we imply that our God cannot do anything either.

In an attempt to refute the quietism of the past, liberals have said "God has no hands but our hands." However, over the course of the years we have discovered that our hands could not fix the problems. Then we came up with a necessary threshold of consensus to bring about the reign of God: the idea of 100 monkeys or 1000 cranes: "let's get 100 of us or fold 1000 cranes." We then discovered if we got one hundred monkeys in a room they would not agree. We don't have powerful hands, and we can't form a consensus, so, if we think God has no hands but our hands, we bury God through a depiction of God as powerless and innocent. The psalmist contradicts our isolation and disingenuous innocence. Our God has hands and arms. A quick look at the psalm indicates that God consistently is the subject of the verb. It seems so unusual that we can talk about a speech having legs, but not God. God has God's very own hands and legs.

In this text God acts by doing marvelous things. The psalmist elaborates with the verbs. God gets the victory; God makes known; and God remembers. There is no clock maker God here.

> *For God comes to judge the earth.*
> *God will judge the world with righteousness*
> *and the peoples with fairness.* (98:9b)

When we hear scholars designate this as an eschatological hymn, our eyes glaze over. We get a sense that we have escaped; it is not our problem. The writer is talking about the "long run." God will come, but not before I retire, or my CD matures. The British economist John Maynard Keynes said "But this *long run* is a misleading guide to current affairs. In the *long run* we are all dead." The word *eschatological* reminds us of the "long run" that comes to pass long after we have already passed.

A preacher once told the story of a board meeting in Hades. It seems they were in the midst of a recruitment campaign; they were brainstorming ideas for growth. A little devil at the end of the table raised his hand and said, "I have done all the right demographic research and discovered a growth strategy that I am sure will work and my research will substantiate" (They talk like that in Hades I am told). "Okay, what is your strategy?" "Well, we have an advertising campaign, and we make commercials for the Olympics and the World Series and the Super Bowl. The message of these commercials is simple. We tell people that all that New Testament eschatological stuff is wrongheaded. Our slogan will be 'Don't worry, there is plenty of time.'"

God has arms and hands beyond our arms and hands. God evokes from us passion if we will but let it happen. God's coming shapes our now. We know God is a way maker because God raised Jesus Christ from the dead and made a way out of our no way.

That prospective student is still sitting in my office. What should we say to him? What should we do?

Psalm 99

The early section of Psalm 99 (99:1–5) begins with the phrase *YHWH mlk* and alternates between theological language, God-talk, and performative language. The psalmist contrasts the reign of God and the appropriate human response, human trembling; as opposed to God's sitting, a sign of stability. Access to stability comes through the process of worship.

The vocabulary clearly indicates the contrast between the human situation and God's experience. The term "tremble" (*rāgaz*) does not occur often in the Psalter (Pss 4:5; Eng 4; 18:8; Eng 7; 77:17, 19; Eng 16, 18), or any other place, for that matter. It occurs in Psalms 18 and 77 as reference to the response of the mountains and the deep before the awesome power of God. The use of the term in Psalm 4 describes a sense of agitation. *Be perturbed/angry, but do not sin* (4:5; Eng 4:4). In all five occurrences the term in the Psalter describes instability before God.

In contrast to the people, the picture of God presented here is a view of stability. The term *yōšēb* ("sitting"; the participle of the verb "to sit" *yāšab*) occurs over one hundred and sixty times in the Hebrew Bible. The term occurs several times in the Psalter (Pss 2:4; 9:8; 9:12; 17:12; 22:4; 29:10; 55:20; 69:26; 80:2; 91:1; 99:1; 102:13). Psalm 17 does not have God as the subject of the sentence; the term refers to adversaries lying in ambush. In Psalm 69 the term refers to the sinners dwelling in their tents. Psalm 91 uses the term to refer to the wise and righteous who dwell in the shelter of the Most High. In the places where the term refers to humans in the Psalter, it conveys a sense of dwelling.

More typically, however, the term assumes God as the subject and in each of these cases (Pss 2:4; 9:12; 22:4; 99:1) the best translation is probably "enthroned." The phrase "enthroned on the cherubim" occurs outside of the Psalter (1 Sam 4:4; 2 Sam 6:2; 2 Kings 19:15; Isa 37:16). In all of these cases, the phrase is a divine *epithet*. An epithet is a noun, adjective, or phrase used to characterize some person or thing. Psalms 99:1 and 80:2 use the phrase "enthroned upon the cherubim," and in these instances as well the term functions as a divine epithet. The epithet describes God's being as enthroned and human existence as agitated.

The use of the image of the cherubim accents the power of God and implicitly underlines the weakness of humans. The cherubim were part of the Temple furniture. Psalms 80 and 99 are the only references to cherubim in the Psalter. They represented the footstool of God, the mercy seat (see Exod 25:17–22; 37:7–9). The cherubim protected the Ark of the Covenant (1 Kings 6:23–28; 8:7). The cherubim were depicted as animals with the wings of an eagle and the body and face of a lion. The people trembled before the LORD who was enthroned on the cherubim, creatures from a cosmic mythology prompting a similar reaction from nature. The earth quakes, a sign of terror and instability.

The repetition of the word "peoples" (99:1–2) makes the same comparison between the stability of God and the instability of humans. In the first occasion of the term the people tremble. In the second occurrence the psalmist uses the term to connote inferiority to God who is exalted over all people.

The statement about God makes a connection to the Zion tradition (99:2). The psalmist connects the reign of God with the place of the elect, Zion. The mention of the cherubim (Ps 99:1) provides a subtle reference to the Temple. Psalm 96 also alludes to the house or sanctuary of God (96:6, 8). Psalm 97 mentions Zion and Judah (97:8). Psalm 99 also mentions Zion (99:2).

The vocation of the people is simple. *Let them praise your great and fearsome name* (99:3). Then the psalmist moves to a formula that breaks up the psalm. *God is holy* (99: 3, 5).

God's strength is described in judicial categories. *The king's power loves justice* (99:4a). The rest of the verse corroborates this affirmation. Like verse 3, verse 5 uses performative language and the affirmation about the holiness of God.

The citation of salvation history (99:6–7), with special mention of Moses and Aaron, finds no parallel in the *YHWH mlk* psalms. The psalmist uses these figures to persuade the audience that the God who has delivered these men of old is about to deliver us (99:8). The task for the present is praise and worship. Hence, the psalm ends with the same sort of performative language that has dominated the piece (99:9).

Shape of the Psalter Issues

The majority of the *YHWH mlk* psalms come from the same section of the Psalter. The theme of the sovereignty of God, as described in these psalms, provides the intellectual core of Book Four which stands as the editorial center of the Psalter.[21]

Book Four answers the problem of the demise of the Davidic power. Using language of creation and foundation of the world, this book points to the LORD as the source of refuge and authorization for any human agency.

From Enthronement to Christology

We all know an enthronement psalm because we sing one every Christmas. Who among us has not sung "Joy to the World," a musical rendition of an enthronement psalm (Ps 96)?

In the black church, enthronement of God refers to the enthronement of the triune God. The enthronement of God is the coming reign of God as well as the present movement of God in history; it is work of the Spirit in the movement of history. The enthronement of the triune God as Christ includes the redemptive work of Christ on the Cross and the anticipatory symbol of Christ outside the empty tomb. Enthronement is a way to get at the mystery of the Trinity.

Humans function as authorized agents only to the degree that they follow the vocation of praise. A vocation of praise means that the self described is not a powerful self, for a powerful self could be self-generated. Rather, it is an authorized self deriving its authority from a relationship with God. With that in mind, we are able to ask about the nature of the authoritative self.

LISTENING IN ON THE ROYAL PSALMS

The Nature of Monarchy

The royal psalms cannot be separated from the ideology of the monarchy for which they provide a literary and liturgical foundation. The king serves as the hero for society at large, and in exchange for this service, the king exercises significant sway over persons and property in antiquity. Even when the monarchy ceased to exist, the function of the monarch as symbol, intermediary, and model remained.[22] The king mediated all power through appointment, wealth, and military threat. He mediated power within the community but also represented the populace to a deity.

The king had three functions in the ancient Near East which are mirrored in the Hebrew Scriptures: First, the king's administration of justice had cosmic impact. Second, the fertility and prosperity of the nation rested in the intermediary powers of the king with God and the just execution of his royal administration. Third, the king's job meant a concern for the underprivileged.[23]

The Shaping and Setting of the Royal Psalms

The king served as hero and model, especially for the landed gentry, but he also served as an intermediary between God and the people. Kingship as a metaphor describes the authoritative self and provides a model for each of us in today's world. The King, as depicted in the royal psalms, provides a guide to the characteristics of the authoritative self.

We are vulnerable. Yet that vulnerability presents us with our greatest strength. The royal psalms often talk about the failure of the king. *All who pass by plunder the king. The king has become a reproach to the neighbors* (89:42; Eng 41).

We are faithful. Spirituality organizes our life. For *who is God except the LORD, and who is a rock, except our God* (18:32; Eng 31).

We are just. Our peace and security depend on it. Much will be given *because the monarch delivers the needy when the needy one calls, the poor, and those with no advocate for them* (72:12).

We are elected. Psalm 2:7b states that *today I have begotten you. Sit at my right hand till I make your enemies your footstool* (110:1). Like Gideon in the wine press trying to thresh wheat, we are elected in a time when the deficit grows large and economic uncertainty continues.

The royal psalms include a number of literary genres and literary perspectives. Three royal psalms are intercessions on behalf of the monarch (Pss 20, 72, 132). Three royal psalms are prayers in the voice of the monarch (Pss 18, 101, 144). Psalms 2 and 110 function as declarations of royal authority.[24]

The Vulnerable King

The idea of a vulnerable king appears elsewhere in the ancient Near East. Ian Engnell points to the dying and rising god image that certain ancient Near Eastern religions ritualized in the inauguration of the monarchs.[25] The story of Sargon depicts him as a child in desperate danger. The same model recurs in the birth of Moses story as well as in the infancy stories in the New Testament.

The idea of the vulnerable leader has modern counterparts as well. The log cabin origins of Abraham Lincoln serve as a validation of his role as a leader who nonetheless, as we would say today, stands in solidarity with the "little guy." Royal laments paint the vulnerability of the king as one of the marks of authenticity worthy of authorization.

Psalm 20

No power exists without God. The authoritative self begins with the awareness of vulnerability because without that awareness a person could imagine agency without an authorizing agent. The royal lament models an expression of vulnerability and power for the authoritative self.

The superscription provides little information to interpret this psalm. Like personal laments, it begins with a plea. The psalmist uses the vocabulary of the personal laments such as the verb "answer" ('ānā(h)). Here however, unlike the personal laments, the psalmist uses this as a plea on behalf of the monarch. *The LORD answer you on the day of trouble* (20:2; Eng 20:1).

The psalmist puts the pleas in the form of wishes or hopes for the monarch. In English grammar a verb that expresses desire is considered to be in the subjunctive mood. In Psalm 20 we encounter a series of subjunctives with God as the subject and the monarch as the object. *May God send . . . may God remember . . . may God grant . . . and may the LORD fulfill . . .* (Ps 20:3–6; Eng 2–5). The subjunctives function as performative language in the context of worship.

The first "I" statement is a statement of trust. *Now I know that the LORD will save God's anointed* (20:7; Eng 20:6). God's responsiveness plays itself out in military/political victory (20:7–10; Eng 6–9) although this may be ritual conflict.[26] We may be seeing here the blending of conflict and vulnerability in the authoritative self. When vulnerability connects with the theme of trust, notice the contrast. *Some of chariots and some of horses (boast), but we boast of the name of the* LORD *our God* (20:8; Eng 20:7). The spatial metaphors present a one up-one down picture. Those who trust in war technology are one down; those who trust in the name of the LORD our God are one up. The king represents us, hence we ask for the king's victory. Indeed the king's victory becomes our victory.

Expressions of trust in the laments derive their power from the assumption of God's authority and sovereignty. At the same time the expression of trust indicates the vulnerability of the monarch.

Psalm 21

Psalm 21 continues the theme of Psalm 20. *In your strength the king rejoices, O* LORD (21:2; Eng 1a). As in the case of Psalm 2, once again in Psalm 21 we get a glimpse of the divine warrior tradition (21:9–11; Eng 8–12). This intercessory prayer on behalf of the monarch does not include any first person speech except the performative language at the end, which is first person plural, "we."

We can see the organic connection between the *YHWH mlk* psalms and the royal psalms. The divine warrior manifests the authoritative reign. The king reigns in vulnerability, serving at the behest of God. If the theological affirmation does not hold true, then the political affirmation likewise is in jeopardy.

Psalm 144

Psalm 144 begins with a blessing of God who enables the king for the conflict/war (144:1). In the *YHWH mlk* psalms, the psalmist takes refuge in God because of God's activity in creation; in this psalm the military power of God provides the rationale for the refuge the monarch takes in God.

The next section (144:3–4) gives an eloquent expression of human vulnerability. *O* LORD *what is a person that you regard him/her, or the child of humans that you think of him/her. A person is like a breath, his/her days are like a passing shadow* (144:3–4).

An expression of vulnerability sets the stage for the psalmist to request God's intervention (144:5–6). The salvation has two aspects. The psalmist asks for deliverance from "the mighty waters" (144:5–6).

This is a traditional image of creation chaos. The mighty waters represent the cosmic conflict and threat. The psalmist also asks for deliverance from the foreigners (*benê nēkor*; 144:7, 11b).

The term *benê nēkor* is, in and of itself, neutral here. While in some cases it connotes impurity (Ezek 44:7), the foreigners who keep the Sabbath are not excluded from the community of faith (Isa 56:6). Foreigners can even benefit from the post-exilic occupational system (Isa 60:10; 61:5). The psalmist gives the reader clues about what type of foreigners these are. These foreigners commit false witness and fraud. The conflict over false witness and fraud is a concern seen in the personal laments. Also like the personal laments, the "I" statements use performative language followed by praise.

The psalmist also uses the language of the *YHWH mlk* psalms. *I will sing a new song* (144:9). Then the psalmist moves back to plea, in fact a repeat of the plea in verse 7, but this time there is a military, rather than a cosmic, threat. *Rescue and deliver me from the hand of foreigners. . . .* (144:11).

The psalmist moves back to performative language. This time, as in the *YHWH mlk* psalms, the performative language uses the subjunctive. What makes the psalmist trust the power behind the performative language is the theological proverb that ends the psalm. The vulnerability of the lament does not drive us to despair because *happy are the people whose God is the* Lord (144:15b).

Psalm 89:38–52

The psalm falls into two sections: the first recounting the election of the Davidic house (89:1–37); and the second lamenting the fall of the Davidic house. We separate these sections for our investigation.

The distinctive superscription, *a Maskil of Ethan the Ezrahite*, provides no information about the setting. This is the only time we find a superscription to Ethan.

The institution of the monarchy is like an old rodeo saddle. It had seen the celebratory times, as well as the spills, that come with agency. "There was this saddle" says a line from a long-defunct television show. In an episode a rich individual, who possessed many fancy and shiny toys, gave the title character an old saddle. Despite his wealth he says, "I don't have much that is worth giving but there was this saddle I used when I used to rodeo." The ability to recount both the adversity of the institution as well as its resiliency in God puts the lie to the myths of innocence and rot at the top.

In a time when Christians in the United States decry slipping attendance and sagging revenues in churches, drifting without hope can become the norm. At a time when clergy misconduct eats away at the credibility of our profession, we can lose sight of the images that brought us to ministry. At times like that we can lament like Psalm 89 and say, "But nevertheless, there was this saddle." The institution of monarchy remains like that saddle—old, scratched but still cherished.

Psalm 89 is a royal psalm which ends Book Three of the Psalter. Closing the collection for the early post-exilic community, it concludes with a statement of the failure of the monarchy and a blessing to the Lord. The passage reminds us of the vulnerability of leadership. The leader and the institutions of leadership experience life as both an authoritative and a vulnerable self. Vulnerability becomes part and parcel of the authoritative self.

The psalm uses the second person, capturing the I-Thou language typical of laments. I-Thou language indicates a close tie between the creator and the created.

Typical of the laments is the language of absence and rejection as seen in the verbs *zānaḥ* ("cast off") and *mā'as* ("reject") (89:39; Eng 38). The verb *'ābar* ("be angry") occurs in the hithpael form, which normally conveys the causative reflexive, which is to say, to cause action on oneself. In human conflict it is like that time when a loved one does something to "push your buttons" and you make yourself angry. The infraction provides a catalyst for an eruption of anger.

God's anger and rejection of the covenant provide a critique of leadership that is ever present. (89:40; Eng 39). God's absence indicates a break in the covenant that the psalmist describes, using the second person, with an accusatory tone. Once again we have three forceful verbs: abhor, defile, and break (89:40, 41; Eng 39, 40).

The term "break" reminds us of the walls of an ancient city that were breached. We can hardly miss the military metaphor, but, at the same time, this text should remind us of the ways in which our own boundaries have been broken. The psalm moves from a military metaphor which modern readers might transform to a psychological metaphor. When one's boundaries or walls come crashing down, the result is intrapsychic and social vulnerability. The verb phrase reminds us of an explosion at a stone wall with the debris of our lives falling everywhere.

When the walls break down, the psalmist tells us what happens: *All who pass by plunder* (89:42; Eng 41). Vulnerability, by its very nature, means that our agency now is circumscribed by others so that all who pass by are unrestrained in their actions toward us.

The enemies rise up and rejoice (89:43; Eng 42). God makes that happen. There seems to be a choreography of status indicated by the verb "exalt" (*rûm*). However, the status derives from God's action not from the caprice of history, according to the psalmist. The psalmist denies the social access of those in good standing with the community.

"Momma said there would be days like this," we cry. Nonetheless, the battered institution continues. But what we remember today is the saddle. It matters little that the saddle has been used for several years or that it has nicks and dings. The leather shows the wear of the elements in places, and the silver cinches do not shine like new. We do not test the leadership of our institutions by their shininess or their absence of lament. Rather, one judges a saddle by its balance, its strength and its softness. Is this the way we should judge our institutions? When we get cynical about the leadership institutions we associate with, remember we are a vulnerable, authoritative self. Remember, there was this saddle.

The Authoritative and Faithful King

Psalm 127

Here we see the king as intermediary, modeling faithfulness to God. The faithfulness of this psalm embodies a sense of election. Psalm 18 amplifies the election in Psalm 2.[28]

The "I" statements in the early part of the psalm recount the trust of the monarch. *I love . . . I take refuge . . . I call upon . . . I am saved.* The first "I" statement of the psalm sets the tone for the entire psalm and particularly verses 2–4; Eng 1–3. *I love you, O LORD, my strength. The LORD is my rock and my fortress and my deliverer. . . .* (18:2–3a; Eng 1–2a).

The verb *rāḥam* ("love") occurs in this form only here in the Hebrew Bible. The statement of confidence and trust reminds us of the beginning of Psalm 21. *O LORD in your strength the king rejoices* (21:2a; Eng 1a).

The literary context surrounds the next "I" statement with metaphors of security (18:3; Eng 2). These metaphors (*my deliverer . . . my God . . . my rock*), lead into the clause *I take refuge* followed by metaphors of military strength (*my shield, and the horn of my salvation, my stronghold*). Amidst this context the psalmist witnesses to dependency on God.

The next two "I" statements come together. *I call upon* and *I am saved* (18:4; Eng 3). These statements connect verses 2–4 (Eng 1–3) to verse 7 (Eng 6). After the section of "I" statements the psalmist recounts the danger (18:8–13; Eng 7–12). The statement of the king's vulnerability creates a narrative tension.

Further, the king's vulnerability mirrors the vulnerability of the non-royal hearers. Just as God delivered the king when *the cords of death encompassed me . . . the cords of Sheol entangled me* (18:5a, 6a; Eng 4a, 5a) so by extension the deliverance of the monarch becomes the deliverance of the nation. The narrative tension is resolved by the appearance of God in verse 7 (Eng 6). The vulnerability catches God's attention. God heard my voice from the context of the temple; my pleas for salvation *went to God's ears*.

The theophany, the appearance of the divine, of these verses depicts the divine warrior. The psalmist continues in such a way as to make the point that the strength of the LORD undergirds the political fortunes of the king. By the time the psalm ends, we hear words of praise and exhortation.

The "punchline" of the psalm occurs in verse 21 (Eng 20). *The LORD rewarded me according to my righteousness*. The monarch should function as the archetype of righteousness. To accent this point the psalmist provides a series of "I" statements of innocence. The first two "I" statements describe a closeness between the monarch and God rooted in righteousness. *For I have kept the ways of the LORD, and I have not done wickedness as to depart from my God* (18:22; Eng 21). Not only did the monarch not pull away from God's will, the psalmist does not push the rubrics of God's will away. *For . . . God's statutes I did not put away from me* (18:23*b*; Eng 22*b*). The first two "I" statements were *kî* clauses. The next two "I" statements represent the result of the conditions set forth by the *kî* clauses. *But I am blameless before God, and I have kept myself from my iniquity.* Then the psalmist takes the reader back to the beginning affirmation of the section, the authorizing function of righteousness. Verses 21–25 (Eng 20–24) begin and end with an affirmation that God gives authority to those who are righteous.

The psalmist makes two politically and theologically important points in this psalm. First, the king must be righteous and second, righteousness has its reward. One might be a powerful self without righteousness, but one can never be an authentically authoritative self without righteousness, for righteousness is the expression of one's self-understanding as authorized by God.

The authorization takes on military clothes. *For by you, I run up to a troop, and by my God, I scale a wall* (18:30; Eng 29).[29] The place of the king and his subjects rests on the doctrine of God. Notice the relationship referred to by the psalmist. *For who is God but the LORD? And who is a rock, except our God? The God who girded me with strength and made my way safe* (18:32–33; Eng 31–32).

The monarch, now authorized by God, says *I pursued my enemies and I overtook them* and *I struck them down* (18:38a, 39; Eng 37a, 38). The authorized pursuit of the enemies results in a thorough defeat for the monarch's opponents. *I beat them fine as dust upon the face of the wind. Like the mud of the streets I cast them out* (18:43; Eng 42).

The result of the authorization outstrips expectations. *People I don't know serve me* (18:44c; Eng 43c). Hence, the appropriate response would be praise, so the last section of the psalm begins with a performative "I" statement. *Therefore I will give you thanks among the nations, O LORD. And I will sing praises to your name* (18:50; Eng 49).

In sum, we note that the authoritative self presented as the monarch includes the expression of vulnerability. However, vulnerability alone does not suffice. Faithfulness substantiates a trust in God as the author of agency. The authoritative self lives only through the mechanism of faith.

The Just King

Two of the royal psalms (72 and 89) provide a conclusion for Books 1 and 2 of the psalter.

Psalm 72

Psalm 72 outlines the king's responsibility for justice followed by a prayer for the king. Just as the king has no power except that given by God through election, so the justice and righteousness of the king come from God (72:1b). However, the prayer declares the king is to carry out his duties in keeping with the rubrics of justice[30] concluding Book Two of the Psalter (72:12–14).

In the entire ancient Near East the understanding that law and justice come from the divine[31] was well known. Psalm 72 refashions these notions into a post-exilic form. Psalm 72 does not have the ancient ring of Psalms 2 and 110; rather we find its closest parallels in Isaiah (9:2–7; 11:1–9).[32]

In the early section we see the theme of intercession. The task of the king requires interceding for the people with God. We notice reciprocity in the two first stanzas. God gives justice prosperity through the king. In each case, the theme of intercession of the king appears.[33] The language of Psalm 72:1 makes it clear that the people can intercede for the monarch.[34] Hence we get the language of hope in the mouth of the psalmist. The writer uses the subjunctive, or optative, expressing desire or hope (a fact we know more from context than grammatical paradigm).

A just king also becomes an authoritative king (72:8–11) as noted in the cosmic, natural element of prosperity. In order to accent this, the writer in verse 3 uses the images of the mountains and hills. In thios instance *šālôm* here refers to prosperity, not just the absence of violence.[35]

The subjunctives and the *kî* (result) clause signal the contingent nature of power. The exercise of power championing the marginal in the community (72:12–14) provides the foundation. The verbs here tell us much concerning the image of the authoritative self and the responsive self. The king delivers (*nāsal*) and saves (*yāša'*), a pro-active depiction. However, the king saves when asked and displays compassion (*ḥûs*). As such, we perceive a responsive picture as well.

The psalmist returns us to the well wishes for the king (72:15–17) and finally the benediction for Book Two of the Psalter (72:18–20).

Psalm 89

The psalm contains two different types of "I" statements. It begins with human performative language typical of prayers for deliverance. *I will sing forever of the loyalty of the LORD. From generation to generation I will make known your faithfulness with my mouth* (89:2; Eng 1).[36] The bulk of the first part of Psalm 89 is also performative language, but it is divine performative language. The interplay between the divine first person (89:4–5; Eng 3–4, 20b-38; Eng 19b-37) and the description of the nature of God in the second person (89:10–14; Eng 9–13) takes on an antiphonal quality which might indicate a liturgical setting of the psalm.[37]

In Psalm 89 we note the lyrical echoes of the prophecy of Nathan (2 Samuel 7)[38] and divine speech which echoes the promise to the Davidic house. However, between the two divine "I" statement sections (89:4–5; Eng 3–4; 89:20b-36; Eng 19b-35), the psalmist places a cosmogony (89:6–19; Eng 5–18), a story of the creation of the universe. We earlier encountered the cosmogony in the *YHWH mlk* psalms but here we have the reign of God via cosmogony and the reign of the monarch through adoption fused together. Cosmogony becomes a witness to the authorizing power of God. The psalmist borrows poetic elements from Near Eastern traditions such as Ugarit, but not to the degree that the monarch is depicted as divine.

The "I" statements point out that the monarch is authorized to rule from the sea to the rivers (89:26; Eng 25); the LORD will function as divine warrior overthrowing the enemies of the monarch (89:23–24); and the LORD has adopted the Davidic monarch as the firstborn son. The byproduct of the adoption is access to God (89:28–29; Eng 27–28).

The "I" statements are all from the monarch's mouth. The monarch here quotes God, in much the same manner we find in Psalm 2. Hence we have the *You said* (Heb 89:20; Eng 19). The authoritative self, as modeled in this royal psalm, has the ability to give witness to authorization. As such, the monarch avoids the myth of innocence.

Psalm 101

In Psalm 101 we can hear the self-disclosing "I" of the monarch. Once again performative language binds the speaker to the words spoken as a vow and a hope which predominate this psalm. *Of loyalty and justice I will sing. To you, O LORD, I will sing* (101:1b; Eng 1). The monarch commits to a course of study. The authoritative self contains an intellectual element; however, the task involves more than the Enlightenment's dispassionate study of ethics and public policy. The challenge and job description of the authorized self equals activism for justice (101:3b). The monarch also commits to a perspective: *I will not set before my eyes base things* (101:3a). A relational view of justice emerges from the text. *My eyes are on the faithful of the land* (101:6a). The monarch promises not to associate with anyone who strays from the ethical path.

The most problematic element in the psalm is its radical naiveté. *Evil I shall not know* (101:4b). Can the authoritative self avoid the knowledge or experience of evil? Can the authoritative self remain innocent? Reinhold Niebuhr would argue that such a position is naive. However, in the politics of race it does point to an interesting dynamic. Any leader who fails the innocence test loses valuable credibility in all other matters.[39] This verse becomes so problematic because the drive to maintain innocence is the root cause for what becomes the myth of innocence.

The Elected King

The king represents our own election. The king is chosen by God; we, as the distant heirs of the king and God, also receive this promise of election. The coronation of the king is probably the context for Psalms 2 and 110 and a reaffirmation of our election. The election of David in 2 Samuel 7 renews the election of the nation,[40] which validates the king's power. The authoritative self emerges out of a context of election and authorization.

Psalm 2

Psalm 2 describes a world in which the authoritative self begins with the conflictual self. *Why do the nations conspire?* (2:1a). Amidst this conflict God's self-assertion includes the authorization of the monarch. In order to accent the point of the conflict, the psalmist brings the adversaries into the room and into the conversation through the use of quotations. *"Let us break their chains," they say "and throw off their fetters"* (NIV 2:3).

Whereas Psalm 89 uses cosmogony language to substantiate God's cosmic rule, Psalm 2 merely refers to the fact of God's cosmic reign in heaven. It describes God as laughing at the foreign rulers much as a large boxer might laugh at a small child trying to punch him only to have arms flailing ineffectively in the air. God laughs, not with a small, embarrassed, coy smile, but with a full, from-the-belly, open-mouthed laugh.

The psalmist connects the election of the monarch and God's selection of Zion as the center of the universe. *I have set my king upon Zion, my holy hill* (2:6). As in Psalm 89, Psalm 2 describes the monarch's recital of the words of God, authorizing the power of the monarch. *You are my son. Today I have begotten you* (2:7b). Psalm 2 describes the election in two ways: military power and adoption, with its concomitant privileges of inheritance. We recall similar resonances in Psalm 89. *I cut a covenant with my chosen one, I swore to David my servant. . . . I will make him my firstborn* (89:4, 28; Eng 3, 27).

After the discussion of election, the psalmist presents us with ritual conflict in which God acts as the warrior (8–9). Next the psalmist pleads for wisdom for Gentile leaders followed by a benediction (2:10–11).

Psalm 110

Like Psalms 2 and 89 the psalmist uses divine first person speech to authorize the monarch. *The LORD says to my lord, "Sit at my right hand until I make your enemies your footstool"* (NRSV 110:1).

The psalmist reminds the monarch that the Lord is at the monarch's right hand (110:5a). Nonetheless, God, as the divine warrior, is the main actor. The psalmist again makes the connection between God and the LORD's anointed.[41]

The picture here is leadership of Gentiles without coercion (110:3). This redefines the nature of power related to the authoritative self. Power in this case is not coercive but rather relational.

Psalm 110, like Psalm 2, brings the themes of the king and Zion together. "The psalm consists of oracles and related declarations of blessing conveyed to the king by a leading priest or prophet."[42] We note the connection between the task of the cultic prophet and the king as models for the community's self-definition.

Summary

The royal psalms make the point that the reign of the faithful Davidic monarch stretches to the whole world. The authorization given by God cannot be invalidated.[43] The worldwide reign of the faithful monarch parallels the theme of the worldwide reign of God in the *YHWH mlk* psalms. Despite mythological borrowing in the psalms, such as in Psalm 89, the monarch remains the adoptee of God and never divine in the Hebrew Bible.[44]

LISTENING IN TO THE EARLY CHURCH

The *YHWH mlk* psalms make use of the divine warrior motif that is later picked up in apocalyptic literature. As we might imagine, the divine warrior imagery ("the kings of the earth" and "rod of iron") was taken over in the Revelation to John (6:15; 17:2; 18:3; 19:19; 21:24; 2:27; 12:5; 19:15).

Vulnerability

The themes of vulnerability and justice intersect in the New Testament picture of Christ in the manger. Matthew 2:11 picks up on the theme of Psalm 72:9–11.

When we consider the trajectory of election, we might plot it out this way: Genesis 12 through Abraham, then Jacob, and then David (2 Sam 7). Psalm 2 expands the Davidic covenant on which Psalm 89 reflects with a bittersweet quality. The New Testament brings this over into the baptism of Jesus and into Romans 12.

The language of adoption recurs in the New Testament (Matt 3:17; Luke 3:21–22; Mark 1:9–11; John 1:31–34). At Jesus' baptism the same adoption language found in Psalm 2 is used. Jesus replaces the king as the symbol of election and the new humanity.

The ancient Near Eastern literature claims that law always comes from a god. When we listen to Matthew 2, we claim that the God who gives us the law is this vulnerable child, Jesus. Without our vulnerable side, we shall never find our capacity for the just.

LISTENING IN TO CONTEMPORARY CULTURE

The sovereignty of God dominates the gospel music scene. When we hear Mahalia Jackson sing "He's Got the Whole World in His Hands," we experience the sovereignty of God the creator that the *YHWH mlk* psalms exude.

From the earliest stage of African American (Christian) sacred music, the ring shout gave witness to the God whose power outstripped the slaveholder's. The ring shout has its closest parallels in the music of African American Pentecostals. The music has moved from the ring shout to Azusa Street, the place in Southern California where the modern Pentecostal movement, including the Church of God in Christ, had its origins.

The Pentecostal music of André Crouch and others testifies to the eschatological dimension of the reign of God. James Cleveland's song "Too Late" makes the point that the imminent reign of God is a theological constant for the African American church. The same point can be said of Mexican American Pentecostals, although not equally as much for all Mexican American Christians. In other words, the centrality of eschatology existed in the slave church from the beginning, and resonates in Mexican American Pentecostalism as well.

The authorizing power of the sovereign God enabled the use of sacred music in the Civil Rights Movement. The God who reigns enabled one to sing, "Ain't gonna let nobody turn me around, turn me around, turn me around." In that regard the sovereign God authorizes human agency.

The theme of agency also plays an important role in the theology and literature of the African American community. Three recent books present African American perspectives on agency: Archie Smith Jr.'s *The Relational Self*; Katie Cannon's *Black Womanist Ethics*; and Darryl Trimiew's *Voices of the Silenced*. Each of these books describes agency of people of color in the United States as being distinctive.

One can also see this distinction when one examines the opening of Richard Wright's novel *Native Son*. The main character, Bigger Thomas, lives in a Chicago tenement with his mother and siblings. In the opening scene of the book, Bigger catches and kills a rat. On the one hand, the scene depicts Bigger's agency. On the other hand, the irony of the scene is that the rat represents Bigger's life: a rat caught in the tenement—one without agency.

Grange Copeland, the main character in the Alice Walker novel *The Third Life of Grange Copeland*, always exercises agency. But he was not an authoritative self in the early part of the novel, for his agency never allowed for the vulnerability that comes with a caring relationship. Only when Grange begins to care about his granddaughter, Ruth, does he become an authoritative self.

Three hallmarks were mentioned earlier for the monarch. First, they behave in a way that affects the cosmos. Second, the result of their behavior is prosperity for the person; sometimes this is psychologized or transformed into benefiting the community. Third, the person demonstrates concern for the underprivileged.

We do not receive compassion from any works of righteousness, or from anything we do. On the one hand, we receive justice from the God who made the universe, the God above all our conceptions of power. But we also receive justice from the God we and the wise pilgrims encounter in the manger, in the stable.

Where does justice come from? It comes from a process of intercession. We see justice in the interplay between the God of power and the God of weakness. When we treat every child as the Christ child, then we will have received the gift of justice.

The agency of the authorized self seeks justice. Therefore the authorized self chooses visibility and agency instead of innocence and invisibility. In his novel *Invisible Man* Ralph Ellison describes in a powerful way the connection between invisibility and lack of agency.

The agency seeking justice involves intercession. This combination of agency, justice, and intercession comes to the fore in Rudolfo Anaya's novel *Bless Me Ultima*. The character Ultima has agency when all those around her seem so caught up in the givenness of the world that they lose their agency—hence becoming invisible. Her visibility in the community comes from her intercession and agency. We see this in her conflict with the *bruja*, the evil magician. She battles the *bruja* twice. The first time she does alone, because even her family refuses to shed their invisibility. Yet her family does join in the second contest, and even though it costs Ultima her life, she does not surrender her agency.

When a time comes in your life that you encounter the man on the park bench who does not look up but simply mutters, "I never vote, it only encourages them," look to your work, evaluate it by the three criteria of the royal psalms, and be encouraged by the validation of the broader community and tradition.

CHAPTER 3

The Contextual Self

Memory and Sanctuary: Singers and Prophets

The Psalter's understanding of the self stands on two legs. First, the awareness of human need expressed in the conflictual self through the personal laments undergirds half of the understanding of the self in the Psalter. Second, the awareness of the authorizing power of the God who reigns and challenges believers to work as authorized agents comprises the other half. This chapter will show how Books Two and Three of the Psalter build on these two legs of the conflictual self and the authorized self, a self that provides a context for the believer, a contextual self.

Books Two and Three bring together three streams of tradition, according to the helpful information of the superscriptions. Three types of superscriptions dominate: the Asaphite; the Korahite; and the Davidic. This mixture combines the streams of personal piety, demonstrated by the Davidic psalms which are largely personal laments, and corporate faith expressed through the official religion practiced by the cultic functionaries, the Asaphites and the Korahites.

The *YHWH mlk* psalms construct a world that evidences God's self-assertion in the cosmos. An authoritative self bases any sense of agency on the challenge of God's self-assertion, and this divine self-assertion takes a number of forms. In the language of the cult officials we find the self-assertion of God in history (the Asaph psalms) and in a holy place (Korahite psalms). The authoritative self finds its root in the authority of God who reigns in history and in the holy place. Therefore, the contextual self grows out of God's initiative of self-assertion and uses place and history as a compass of identity, a compass for the self.

The Structure of Books Two and Three of the Psalter

The first section of Book Two of the Psalter begins with the Korahite psalms (42–49) and ends with an orphan Asaph psalm (Ps. 50). The remainder of the psalms of Book Two are attributed to David (Pss 51–72).

The Korahite and the Asaphite groups were functionaries of the official religion representing cultic prophets and singers. Book Three of the Psalter seems to be largely a collection of the psalms of clergy and official religion. Book Three begins with the Asaphite Booklet. All but two (Pss 86, 89) of the psalms in Book Three come from either the collections of the Asaph psalms (Pss 73–83) or the Korahite psalms (Pss 84–85, 87–88).

Religious functionaries in antiquity played a major role in social construction. While the monarch brought about order and interceded with God on behalf of the community, the religious functionaries (i.e., priests, prophets, and singers) did much the same task using a different power base.

The cultic prophets performed two functions. They provided oracles to the nation or individuals in time of crisis, and they provided intercession in times of national or personal crisis. This group functioned as a cultural elite having received the spirit through the power of religious experience. They lost their personal identity as well as their language which was replaced by the language of the divine. Hence, when we find first person speech in these texts, it is divine first person speech.

Boundaries between priests and prophets are blurry. The so-called prophetic psalms exhibit certain characteristics. One is the role of promise, typically expressed in the form of a quotation of an oracle from God and extrapolated with the divine first person. Certain moral conditions must arise for the promise to be fulfilled.

Books Two and Three incorporate a fourfold structure. The first cycle of Korahite psalms begins the piece (Pss 42–49). The second movement, the Davidic psalms (Pss 51–72), is preceded by the orphan Asaph psalm (50). Then the Asaph psalms constitute the third movement (Pss 73–83), closing out the Elohistic psalter (Pss 42–83). Finally, the second Korahite cycle (Pss 84–88) provides an appendix to the Elohistic psalter.[1]

Books Two and Three present a contextual self derived from God's assertion in history (memory) and place (Zion). Having a sense of history (memory) and place (Zion) is the basis for defining this self as the contextual self. The Korahite psalms distinctively lift the role of history and Zion in the faith of the people. These are psalms of memory and re-memory.

Re-memory is the process of coming to terms with traumatic memories. I borrow this term, created as it were by Toni Morrison, because it captures the verb and noun quality of a historical self. In her novel, *Beloved,* the ghost Beloved is the embodiment of Sethe's memory of the trauma she suffered. If the character Sethe does not go through the process of re-memory, she is condemned to live the rest of her life with the ghost Beloved. The historical task of the contextual self forces one to come to terms with history or be haunted by it. Amnesia and nostalgia merely pretend that the ghost is not there.

The Elohistic Psalter

The Elohistic psalter (Pss 42–83) is derived from a preference for the divine appellation Elohim. This section, spanning the entirety of Book Two and most of Book Three, uses the divine name, Elohim, which is often associated with the Northern Kingdom.

LISTENING IN TO THE KORAHITE SONGS OF ZION

Gunkel designated six psalms as songs of Zion: Pss 46, 48, 76, 84, 87, and 122. Notice that the Korahite psalms include four songs of Zion (Pss 46, 48, 84, 87). Of the songs of Zion three bear witness to prophetic influence in the shaping of the language (Pss 46, 48, and 76). The Asaph and Korahite psalms make up the entire collection of the songs of Zion (with the exception of Psalm 122). The distinctive voice of the Korahites reminds us to pay attention to placement and displacement.

A Sense of Placement and Displacement

A sense of place presents an interesting constellation for African American, Mexican American, and Japanese American literature, in that the theme of place makes eloquent appearance throughout the literature of these groups, from *Cane* to *The Floating World* and *Farewell to Manzanar*. In these rather typical novels we see how every sense of placement carries a corollary of displacement.

In his novel *Cane*, the African American writer Jean Toomer explores the ideas of placements and displacement. By using two locations (Washington D.C. and rural Georgia), he captures the plight of the modern person. This modern-day person, through a sense of displacement, suffers both from a loss of initiative and from a desire to conform, fed by a growing materialism. As the African American slaves left the South, according to Toomer, a disorientation overcame their sense of humanity.[2]

In her novel *The Floating World*, Cynthia Kadohata describes the life of an itinerant Japanese American family through the eyes of a young girl growing to adulthood. She lives in a world that floats as her family drives through the West in search of work and destiny. Her sense of placement was in fact displacement.

Another Japanese American writer, Jeanne Wakatsuki Houston, chronicles her family's transition from placement to displacement due to the illegal internment of Japanese Americans during the Second World War in the book *Farewell to Manzanar*. For these writers, placement and displacement form the ever-present dialectic of life.

The Mexican American writer Sandra Cisneros captures this sense in her work *The House on Mango Street*. "But what I remember most is moving a lot. Each time it seemed there were more of us. . . ."[3] Placement finds its semantic range amidst the furniture of displacement, moving. "The house on Mango Street is ours, and we don't have to pay rent to anybody, or share the yard with the people downstairs, or be careful not to make too much noise, and there isn't a landlord banging on the ceiling with a broom. But even so, it's not the house we thought we'd get."[4] Cisneros reminds us that the sense of place often includes a sense of displacement.

Toni Morrison makes the same point in a number of her novels. The novel *The Song of Solomon* describes the Mercy Hospital that had no mercy. The novel *Beloved* describes a place called "Sweet Home" that was neither sweet nor home. By underlining the false sanctuaries we inhabit, Morrison invites the reader to a sense of re-placement. The sense of re-placement exchanges the false sanctuary for the real refuge. In the face of displacement, one might reach for the artificial re-placement instead of embracing true placement.

The Zion songs, distinctive voice of the Korahites, describe God's self-assertion in the place Zion. However, this assertion does not lead to a narrow chauvinism, but rather to an awareness of placement and displacement. The Zion songs provide their own critique of an idolatrous sense of placement.

Psalm 46

God is our refuge and our strength
Very often found help in times of trouble
Therefore we will not fear,
though the earth change and
though the mountains move in the heart of the seas. . . .
There is a river whose streams make glad the city of God,
the holy habitation of the Most High (46:2–3, 5; Eng 1–2, 4).

Here we have a familiar psalm which provided Martin Luther the inspiration for his hymn "A Mighty Fortress Is Our God." Luther renders a rather paraphrastic translation in the first line of the hymn: "A mighty fortress is our God, a bulwark never failing." Today's English Version translates the text as *God is our shelter and strength always ready to help in times of trouble* (GNB 46:1). "Very present" or "well proved help in trouble" is the NRSV rendering of the passage (NRSV 46:1). The discussion which follows will be framed in terms of this awareness of God's strong, sheltering presence.

Psalm 46 has three parts. It begins with a description of our dependence on God. The dependable God enables us to remain sanguine in the midst of turmoil, even turmoil on a cosmic scale such as earthquake and typhoon. Earthquake and typhoon are typical ancient Near Eastern mythological images.[5] They echo the *YHWH mlk* psalms such as Psalm 93. The first section introduces the sense of disequilibrium and the term *selah* indicates the seams accurately: 2–4, 5–8, 9–12; Eng 1–3, 4–7, 8–11.

The second section presents a picture of opposites. The equipoise of God contrasts to the ever shifting situation of nature and the enemies of God. Once again, the psalmist uses the connecting idea of water. However, instead of the "tumultuous waters of chaos" (*mêmāyw*), of verse 4 (Eng 3) we find in the second stanza a reference to "river" (*nāhor*, 46:5; Eng 4). This theme probably derives from Canaanite mythology in which the high god El was associated with the river. El's throne stands at the head waters of two streams.[6] Now God replaces the image of El.

As in the "Song of the Sea" (Exod15), the enemies of God are thrown into the chaos, into the waters, and the people of God find a place for sanctuary. This psalm stands midway between the oldest strata of Hebrew poetry and the classical expression of the Zion hymns.[7] We notice a shift as the image of water changes from doom to stability and refreshment, prompting the reader to connect this psalm with the first Korahite psalm (Ps 42) which mentions thirst.

The psalmist leads the reader to contemplate the presence of God in the place. The psalmist uses a number of phrases to make this point including *the holy habitation of the Most High* (46:5; Eng 4) and *God is in the midst of her* (46:6; Eng 5). The cosmic turmoil of verses 3–4 (Eng 2–3) finds a parallel in the political turmoil of verse 7 (Eng 6). Here we note the hymn of praise influenced by the prophetic sensibilities.[8] The presence of God equals the help of God. The section ends with a statement of confidence.

The expression *the God of Jacob* parallels *the LORD of hosts* (46:8; Eng 7). This might make the claim that the epithet, the God of Jacob, signals a northern text more problematic.[9] Whether the material is northern or not, Zion provides a refuge based on the authority of God. The psalmist used precise "refuge" language that will occur again in Psalm 48.[10]

An imperative,*Come, behold the works of the LORD*, begins the next section (46:9; Eng 8). The end of the stanza returns to the imperative. *Be still, and know that I am God* (46:11; Eng 10). Stuhlmueller provides an interesting translation of this verse:*"Be still and experience how I am God!"*[11] The psalmist uses the term, *yāda'*, which means "to know and to experience." Two descriptive clauses concerning the nature of God as exalted follow this instruction and then the psalm returns to the theme of the previous stanza, God with us. The psalmist glorifies the city because she has a dynamic connection with God.[12]

As noted above, there are connections to the prophetic literature in this psalm. The presence of the first person speech by the divine (46:11; Eng 10) parallels the Yahweh speech used in prophetic texts.

We should note the twofold response to the speech of God: God raises nations, political entities, as well as the earth, the cosmic entity. The Zion theme here connects to the expression of God's self-assertion in creation.[13]

Psalm 48

Great is the LORD *and exceedingly to be praised*
    in the city of our God
    ... the city of the great King
God, within her citadels reveals God as a sure refuge.
For behold, the kings assembled and they came on together, They
saw. . . .

The second song of Zion gives an internal signal regarding the structure of the psalm. The term *selah* occurs in verse 9 (Eng 8) cutting the psalm more or less into two (48:2–9; Eng 1–8 and 48:10–15; Eng 9–14). The first half, bisected by the *kî* clause, depicts the power of God over the nations. The psalm begins with a description of the grandeur of Zion (the place of God) then blends in themes of the reign of God ("the great king").

Connecting the two parts of the first section is the theme of revelation. The self-revelation of God, located in the citadel of Zion, provides a refuge (48:4; Eng 3). When the royal opponents collect themselves, they perceive Zion, not simply as a city or even a citadel, but as the citadel of God.

This perception changes the effect of the opponents, who react in panic. The psalmist connects this to the tradition of the holy war. The term for panic (*bāhal*) occurs most notably in the "Song of the Sea" (Exod 15:15), an ancient example of Hebrew victory hymn following holy war. The other occurrences of the term in Hebrew narrative refer to the panic of the Hebrews (see Judg 20:41; 1 Sam 28:21; 2 Sam 4:1). The term also occurs in other places in the Psalter but usually with the same meaning (Pss 6:11; 30:8; 48:6; 83:18; 90:7).

The idea of enemies writhing like a woman in childbirth occurs in Isaiah (13:8; 21:3). Interestingly enough these parallels are in oracles against Babylon. The Zion song here blurs the security of God and the security of Zion presupposed in the earlier tradition.[14]

The second half of Psalm 48 describes the meditation of the psalmist in the midst of the temple (48:10; Eng 9) which is an important location for revelation. The intersection of the presence of God and this specific place provides the theological compass for the psalmist. The psalmist creates a parallel structure in the two contrasting sections. The first section describes Zion, then the pagan royals. The second section describes God and then the pious pilgrims. In this section the psalmist prescribes behavior and proffers a set of instructions (48:13–14; Eng 12–13). The instruction is for Zion to be glad (48:12; Eng 11). Then we find an instruction to the daughters of Judah to rejoice. However, the psalmist provides us a rationale introduced by the *lĕmāʿan* ("for the sake of") and *mišpāṭêkā* ("your judgments"). The language here points to the double address of this psalm. On the one hand, the psalmist directs the speech to an audience; on the other hand, God provides the psalmist a listening ear, and hence the use of the second person verb.

> *Walk about Zion,*
> *surround it,*
> *count its towers.*
> *Consider well its ramparts*
> *. . . for the sake of telling the next generation,*
> *"This is God,*
> *our God forever and ever.*
> *God will be our guide for all time."*
> (48:13–14a, 14c-15; Eng 12–13a, 13c-14)

The imperative, walk about, seems to be directed to the audience. The goal of the "walk about" is an infectious confidence in God and Zion (48:14–15; Eng 13–14). Zion remains an outward and visible symbol of the presence of God.

The Christian lectionary places Psalm 48 in the liturgical context of Whitsunday (or Pentecost) which grew out of the celebration of the Feast of Weeks, an agricultural feast to celebrate the harvest (Exod 23:16; 34:22). Appropriating the psalm in this way makes sense because the Christian celebration of Pentecost celebrates the palpable presence of the Spirit (Acts 2). The particularity of Zion in Judaism resonates with the particularity of the *incarnation* of God in Jesus for Christians.[15]

Instructing coming generations is the explicit purpose of this psalm. The present visible symbol of refuge becomes the interpretive guide for the future. For indeed, these specifics shape a believing community.

Psalm 84

The sense of placement and displacement takes an interesting turn in Psalm 84, moving from a sense of place to a sense of peoplehood or ecclesiology.

In John Milton's classic *Paradise Lost* there is speech that could have come from almost any North American context today: "To reign is worth ambition though in hell; Better to reign in hell than serve in heaven." To refute Milton's claim, to negate the asertion that the self must be first at all costs, is to move toward an ecclesiological understanding of human community.

Garry Wills, in his book *Certain Trumpets,* remarks that there are thousands of books on leadership and not many on followership. By followership I mean life beyond the ambitious will to power which can be found even in the small politics of a family. For instance, the will to power may exhibit itself in such a mundane thing as who controls the remote control to the television.

The first two stanzas of the psalm begin with an awareness that the Temple was a special place. The psalmist gets at the transformative power of the place in three ways. First the psalmist comments on the beauty of the Temple with the term, *yādîd* ("lovely") which occurs eight times (Deut 33:12; Isa 5:1; Jer 11:15; Pss 45:1 and superscription; 60:7; Eng 5; 84:2; Eng 1; 108:7; Eng 6; 127:2) in the Hebrew Bible. The term usually refers to the object of affection, namely the "beloved." When the NRSV translates the term as "lovely," one should understand the interface of the projection of beauty onto the object of our affection, the process by which an object is named "lovely."

Second, the psalmist describes the Temple as a place for which believers long. The very being of the believer desires the Temple to the point of fainting. The word for "long" or "desire" finds its closest parallel in the same term used to describe Jacob's homesickness for his father's house.

Third, the psalmist describes the Temple as a home. Just as the birds have nests, so the believer has the Temple. God's house becomes our home as the psalmist blends the experience of being a guest in God's house and being at home.

This stanza closes with the affirmation that God is our God but also our monarch. As such, the reign of God continues to undergird the sense of placement and displacement.

Being in a certain place generates a certain type of person; a person generated in this place is happy. The formula "happy is . . ." occurs in some nineteen psalms (Pss 1, 2, 32, 33, 34, 40, 41, 65, 84, 89, 94, 106, 112, 119, 127, 128, 137, 144, 146), generally as an indication of the "good life." Often, as is the case here, the term introduces a participial clause describing the desired behavior. *Happy are those who dwell* (yôšbê) *in your house . . . happy is the person whose strength is in you. . . .* (84:5, 6; Eng 4, 5) Just dwelling in a particular place shapes behavior.[16]

Dwelling in God's house, for the psalmist, parallels praising. Singing praise is formative for the psalmist, and the place brings out spontaneous music which shapes the singer and the audience.

The happy one also acknowledges God as the authorizing power. How are these happy people transformed? The person generated by the sacred place generates things as well. This person brings moisture to an otherwise dry place and moves from strength to strength (see 84:7–8a; Eng 6–7a).

The psalmist ends this stanza with an affirmation parallel to the affirmation in verse 4b; Eng 3b. The first affirmation made use of the monarch language to accent the reign of God; this time the psalmist uses the language of the high god concept from the ancient Near Eastern literature affirming that *the God of gods will be seen in Zion.*

For a day in your courts is better
than a thousand elsewhere.
I have chosen to stand at the threshold
in the house of my God
than live in the tents of the wicked. (84:11; Eng 10)

The one who stands at the threshold is not a bouncer but a door-keeper. A bouncer throws people out. A doorkeeper is like a bell captain who stands at the hotel entrance and helps the weary travelers with luggage as we struggle in and out.

"Tents of the wicked" differ from the NRSV translation "tents of wickedness" because the issue is ecclesiological, not merely a matter of person ethics. The person has no option to embrace an Enlighten-ment neutrality. One is either in the Temple or in the tents of the wicked, a term which connotes the adversaries. The contextual self reminds the conflictual self that without the rooting in the Temple, the sacred space, we lose our identity and become the adversary.

For the Christian community, Jesus functions as a doorkeeper. Contrary to Miltonian followership, there is something in this trans-formative place onto which the believer holds tenaciously: the provi-dence of God. The psalmist returns us to language describing the generosity of God through the metaphor of the sun which makes agriculture possible. The psalmist brings the reader to the theme of the protection of God through the reference to the shield. However, the benefits of God's favor, honor, and every good thing come to *those who walk uprightly.* Here we have a metaphor for ethical life in the community.

The authorized self can succumb to the will to power, but the contextual self provides an ecclesiology quite different. When we as a community of authorized selves find ourselves embroiled in con-flict or stress, the psalmist would have us count to ten and repeat "I would rather be a doorkeeper in the house of my God than live in the tents of the wicked."

The psalmist concludes with *Happy is the person who trusts in you.* (84:13; Eng 12) Ultimately the Zion tradition builds on the authoriz-ing God who protects and nurtures.

Psalm 87

God founded the city on the holy mountains
The LORD loves the gates of Zion
>>*more than all the dwelling places of Jacob*
>>*honorific things are said of you,*
O city of God.
I mention Rehab and Babylon among those who know me
Behold Philistia and Tyre with Cush,
they say, "This one was born there."
And of Zion it shall be said,
>>*"This person or that person was born in it."*
For the Most High will establish her.
The LORD keeps count in registering the peoples,
"this one was born there."
and singers as well as the pipe-players say,
"All my springs are in you."

Psalm 87 contains two movements. First, the psalmist affixes God's love on Zion, a city with a good foundation, the holy mountains. What makes the place special is God's love for it—a love that surpasses even the love for the places of other elect communities, such as Jacob's.

The second movement, which begins with verse 4, shifts to the divine first person. God causes us to remember, mention. The psalmist uses the Hebrew verb *zākar* ("to remember"). The verb form here is a hiphil which is a causative form, so the verb is rendered in a wooden way "to cause to remember or remind." In a more colloquial way this becomes "to mention." God mentions that Gentile cities, such as Babylon and Tyre, acknowledge the power of Zion through the issue of birthright. The second movement focuses on the issue of birthright.

The psalmist put into the mouth of Gentiles a confession of the importance of birth in Jerusalem (87:5). The location of the birthplace serves an authorizing function. Zion itself is an authorizing birthplace, created and protected by God. Indeed, God keeps a record of those born in this "right" place.

After the selah, normally understood as a seam, we find an interesting postscript shifting the focus from a narrow authorization of those who can claim a Zion birthplace to a broader election. In other words, all people everywhere find their origins in Zion.

Psalm 76: an Asaphite Zion Song

In Judah God is known,
God's name is great in Israel;
God's abode has been established in Salem,
God's dwelling place in Zion (76:2–3; Eng 1–2).

We see the theme of God's presence as the authorizing element for the importance of Zion in the Zion songs, including Psalm 76. This presence includes God's activity in the founding of Zion. Related to the matter of God as founder and continuing presence in Zion, God functions as protector of Zion. This Zion song makes abundantly clear that God has the power over human military might.

God's founding, ongoing presence and protection should generate a type of behavior. *Make your vows and perform them to the* LORD *your God* (76:12; Eng 11). In other words, God's authorizing power and self-assertion in terms of place elicits a believing community that receives placement and displacement relative to behavior. Zion becomes a metaphor for the reign of God that critiques all other exercises of power. The experience of placement and displacement is the arena for the exercise of power.

Summary of the Zion Songs

Far from falling into a narrow parochialism, the Zion songs forge a critique of idolatrous identity. God provides the sole appropriate source of authority. As such, the Zion songs build their own radical critique of the very official religion that gave them birth.[17]

The contextual self depends on the visible symbol of Zion and the intellectual symbol of memory as ways to name the presence of God. The presence of God is as central in the theological formulation of the contextual self as the absence of God is in the development of the conflictual self.

LISTENING IN TO THE EARLY CHURCH

The strongest echo of the Zion Songs is found in the Revelation to John. In the opening of the sixth seal, the people seek refuge and become so desperate that they call out to the natural world, the rocks of the mountains, around them, *Fall on us and hide us from the face of the one seated on the throne and from the wrath of the Lamb; for the great day of their wrath has come, and who is able to stand?* (NRSV, Rev 6:16–17).

Typically New Testament scholars notice the use of the Day of the LORD tradition (Isa 2:12–21) presupposed in the Revelation text.[18] The rhetorical question, "who can stand?" occurs in Psalm 76:8 (Eng 7), and also in prophetic books (Joel 2:11, 31b; Zeph 2:2; Nah 1:6).[19] Both the psalm passage and the opening of the seal celebrate the ultimate exercise of the reign of God. The Revelation passage introduces the section that describes those who will be spared (Rev 7:1–17), namely the church.

The reference to the river that makes glad the hearts of those who love the LORD in Psalm 46:5 (Eng 4) echoes the river of the Water of Life in Revelation (22:1). This same metaphor occurs in prophetic material (Ezek 47:1; Zech 14:8) and Johannine material (John 4:10, 14). In all of these cases the metaphor has eschatological overtones.

The term "Zion" itself occurs seven times in the New Testament (Matt 21:5; John 12:15; Rom 9:33; 11:26; Heb 12:22; 1 Pet 2:6; Rev 14:1). In each of these occasions the passage accents the specific revelation in Jesus and the eschatological implications of Zion. Similarly, the Zion songs talk about the specific revelation of God in Zion and serve as the vehicle for the transformation of the world. In the New Testament, Zion becomes inextricably bound to the person of Christ; as such it is a place with implications for the end of time.

LISTENING IN TO CONTEMPORARY CULTURE

When we hear the Dixie Hummingbirds sing "Zion Used to Moan," we hear the combination of the spatial and temporal elements of Zion in African American liturgy and theology. The song describes the "old time church" with a fondness. When the world changed, or more to the point when the church changed, "then things got bad."

Zion is a place of orientation. When African Americans sing "We are Marching to Zion," the eschatological and justice elements of the song are unmistakable. Zion remains a place that critiques this place. Therefore, Zion takes on eschatological overtones. Just as heaven becomes a metaphor for the full reign of God, so does Zion.

Therefore, we should not be surprised that the sanctuary in Morrison's novel *Beloved* is the "Clearing" and not an official authorized building. Likewise, in the Anaya novel *Bless Me, Ultima*, the sacred place was the mountains and the plains as well as the church building. Zion becomes the place where one resists the present order.

LISTENING IN TO THE ASAPHITE PSALMS

The Asaphites, who originated the core of this material, come from the northern kingdom designated Israel or Ephraim. The Chronicler's tradition would indicate that these were temple singers: "On that day David first appointed that thanksgiving be sung by Asaph and his colleagues" (1 Chr 16:7). According to the Chronicler, during the post-exilic period there existed a strong interest in sacred music. It seems singing had grown into a major element in liturgy.[20] The geographical location of the Asaphites presents problems. First Chronicles 6 locates both Asaph and Korah in the northern kingdom, while Numbers 26:58 indicates that Korah was in Judea.[21]

Book Three of the Psalter opens with an Asaph psalm. The Asaph collections include Psalm 50 and Psalms 73–83. All of this comes from the Elohistic psalter (Pss 42–83), that group of psalms that uses Elohim, instead of Yahweh, as the name of God.

The Bible tells us: *Moreover, David appointed certain of the Levites as ministers before the ark of the LORD, to invoke, to thank and to praise the LORD, the God of Israel. Asaph was the chief. . . .* (1 Chr 16:4–5a). We do not have a way to confirm the Chronicler's claims of a connection to an eponymous Asaph with Levitical background.[22]

However, an examination of the content of the Asaph psalms more likely leads to the conclusion that Asaphites functioned as cultic prophets. Such a discovery presents no major conflict with the Chronicler. First Chronicles 25 makes the connection between the temple singers and their ancestors who were described as prophets. The process of cultic prophecy indicates that this material might, in fact, fit into a model of prophetic activity in Ephraim. Hence, these may be psalms out of the Ephraimite tradition stream.[23]

Religious professionals functioned as keepers of the tradition(s). They used the language of memory to carry out their assigned duties. During the period of the Chronicler, we find three groups of singers: Asaph; Heman; and Jeduthun. The Asaph group came first, but their primacy ended not long after the period of the Chronicler.[24]

The Chronicler claims an Ephraimite origin for the Asaphites, and the linguistic material supports such a conclusion. The form and function of the material corroborate such a designation, if only tentatively. Nonetheless, we see a group of religious professionals managing memory for the sake of the community.

"The question at issue in the cult is whether God will continue to act in Israel's behalf as he did in the past or withdraw his aid because of her disobedience."[25] This question remains, as our role and identity are informed by God's revelation. We resonate with the psalmist who says, *but when I thought how to understand this, it seemed to me as a wearisome task* (Ps 73:16, NRSV).

At first look the Asaph psalms appear to be an eclectic collection. The voice of the individual sets up the tone of the psalmist (Ps 73). The editor includes collective laments (Pss 74, 79, 80, 83) as well as prophetic psalms (Pss 50, 75, 81, 83)[26] and a historical recital (Ps 78). Psalm 76 is the only song of Zion in the collection, and Psalm 77 is the only personal lament. The form critical designation of Psalm 82 is difficult to pin down. It has similarities to the *YHWH mlk* psalms as well as the prophetic psalms, but the distinctive voice of the Asaphite psalms resonates when we hear their call to re-memory.

Toward Re-memory

Three scenarios help us understand the issue of history, memory, and re-memory.

First Picture

One day during class, a comment in a book that argued that African Americans present a distinctive American experience because of slavery distressed a Euro-American student. He asked, "Did not every immigrant group suffer?" His concern revolved around the issue of moral superiority. The African American professor felt an immediate visceral response and backed away. In order to address the question, she would have to come to terms with the history of slavery in the U.S. Both the African American professor and the Euro-American student wanted to escape a common threat—the past.

Henry Ford once said, "History is bunk!" We should not find this surprising. When Anne Wilson Schaef describes North American culture as addictive, she points out the lack of memory in the culture.[27] One element of the addictive nature of society expresses itself in a feckless forgetfulness, a myopic memory, and a narcotic nostalgia. While this combination provides a potential for relative social stability, it short-circuits matters of theodicy, our complaints with God.

Second Picture

A class in sexual ethics had gotten off to a good start. The course included a discussion of sexuality, violence, and abuse. For the first few weeks, after the class discussion, persons approached the teachers with memories of abuse that arose bit by bit, set off by the class material. How dare these professors spark the process that Toni Morrison calls "re-memory"!

Third Picture

The same themes of memory and re-memory run throughout contemporary literature. Toni Morrison's novel *Beloved* and Pat Conroy's novel *The Prince of Tides*, to name just two, deal with memory. Conroy, who grew up in an abusive family, told an interviewer that he writes as part of the excavation of his personal history and memory. Likewise, the psalter pays attention to memory. The question before us is, "Why and how do we dare re-memory?"

History, memory, and re-memory create a catch-22. If we do not remember, we do not live. Rather we fall into rebellion (Ps 106:7). *They did not remember the abundance of your steadfast love, but rebelled against the Most High at the Red Sea* (106:7b, NRSV). On the other hand, if we do remember, we must wrestle with the ghosts of memory.

The dominant culture in contemporary North America has exchanged the life of re-memory for a death-dealing drug, a falsely managed past. This dominant culture vacillates from amnesia to narcotic nostalgia. Such a position allows us to escape the responsibility of history by flattening history in favor of a valorization or demonization of the past.

In antiquity the task of memory and history fell not to university professors but to the court historians, cultic prophets, and singers who used song to rehearse the history of the people.

Bookends: Psalm 73 and 83

We can think of Psalms 73 and 83 as bookends. Psalm 73 reads like a wisdom lament; Psalm 83 petitions God for deliverance. Psalm 73 does not play as much with the theme of remembrance as subsequent psalms but gives a tone that continues within Book Three. The themes of Psalm 73 echo Psalms 1 and 2, so much so that one might understand Psalm 73 as a summary of Psalms 1–72.[28] The trauma of a "near miss" provides the context for the reflection of remembrance.

> *Truly, God is good to Israel, to those who are pure in heart.*
> *But as for me, my feet almost stumbled,*
> *My steps had nigh well slipped.*
> *Because I was envious of the arrogant,*
> *The peace/prosperity of the wicked I saw.* (73:1–3)

The "I" statements early in this psalm recount feelings based on perceptions: *I was envious* and *when I saw.* Psalm 73 opens up the spiritual dissonance, and often concomitant temptation, of the people of faith. God mediates the dissonance which life and faith create. God's loyalty resolves the discord as much as it is possible in human existence. Hence the final "I" statement of this section says, *I went . . . then I perceived.* (73:17)

This psalm blends lament and confession. Psychologists have an apt term for the situation of the post-exilic hearer of the psalm, "cognitive dissonance." When we encounter two ideas that contradict, but are forced together in our experience, we have cognitive dissonance. A movement from its creation to meditation and to resolution of dissonance travels through the psalm. The cultic prophet uses it as a prelude to remembrance. The psalmist slyly creates discord by beginning with a taken-for-granted affirmation of faith.

Truly, God is good to Israel, to those who are pure in heart. The psalm begins with an affirmation of the goodness of God which frames the entire psalm and possibly the entire book of the Psalter. Further, it frames the dissonance for the psalm and the book.

Next we hear the confession, *But as for me, my feet almost stumbled, my steps had well nigh slipped,* noting the qualified nature of this confession. We have made confessions like these. In fact, those are often some of the easiest confessions to make; these confessions we share with others about how we came close to the fall. We can relate to the country and western song "Almost Persuaded." "I almost lost my temper." "I almost ate that food I wasn't supposed to." Nonetheless, we take this confession of "almost" seriously. For we recall Cain, who crossed over and was no more. We recall Judas, who crossed over and was no more. We recall Peter, who crossed over, but Jesus saved.

The situation for the dissonance arose when the psalmist envied the *šĕlôm* of the wicked. The term *šĕlōm* translates into English as "prosperity" and carries the connotation of the absence of violence and the presence of economic well-being. Psychological well-being is also alluded to, as much as is possible in the ancient world. However, the idea of prosperity and peace of mind for the wicked create a cognitive dissonance for the believer.

Who are the wicked? These people have sound and sleek bodies. They manage to stay out of trouble, yet they party hard. They have tongues full of hurtful words. They scoff at the very values that Scripture has us cherish (73:4–5).

We want everyone else to get what they have coming, especially the wicked. Fred Craddock tells the story of a little girl who cheated on her Spanish homework, only to be rewarded later by receiving an award for Spanish. The story makes us want to scream "Stop, this is not fair!"

Instead, our enemies all too often reap beauty, wealth and privilege. In the movie *Teacher's Pet* Clark Gable wanted to enchant Doris Day. However, the narrative tension in the movie complicated this romance. One element of complication was the Doris Day character's prior love interest. Gable's character hoped that Day's love interest would be ugly, poor, stupid, or "something disenchanting." But he turned out to be Gig Young, an attractive, intelligent, warm sort of fellow. What can you do when the wicked are good-looking and charming? The psalmist draws a picture of a world where the enemies all too often prosper. Often the wicked present us with comely appearances or seductive power, as is the case with the ghost Beloved, who irresistibly attracts Sethe in *Beloved*.

The next group of "I" statements describes the innocence of the psalmist. The dissonance comes through again, as ethical action is of no benefit.

> *To no effect,*
> *I have kept my heart clean,*
> *washed my hands in innocence.*
> *But I am afflicted all day long.*
> *I am rebuked every morning.*
>
> *If I had said, "I will speak thus,*
> *'Behold the generation of your children!'"*
> *I would have acted treacherously.*
> *But when I thought how to understand this,*
> *a wearisome task it (was) in my eyes.*
> *Until I went into the sanctuary of God,*
> *then I perceived their end.* (73:13–17)

Since the psalmist found previous action ineffective, duplicity as a strategy is dismissed and dissonance is mediated only through worship. We hear the psalmist express this in verse 16. We discover here three key terms expressed in the first person: *ḥāšab* ("to think, consider"); *da'at* ("to know"); and *bĕ'en* ("to understand"). To think and contemplate point to a reflective process. To know likewise exhibits an experiential dimension. Understanding comes from the ability to see distinctions; it conveys the ability to separate things. "Perceived" probably captures the separating theme in the text of Psalm 73.[29]

Worship provides the necessary revelation in this passage. The problem and its dissonance demonstrates some of the mystery of God and history. Worship presents the only refuge for this kind of dissonance. We do not find answers; we find the presence of God.

This text reminds us of the climax of the book of Job (41–42) when God did not answer Job's questions. God however, did something much better than answer questions; the very presence of God was given. In verse 17 of Psalm 73 the psalmist gives two clues to the importance of God's presence as symbolized in the sanctuary. The verse begins with "until," undoing the frustration recounted in the previous section of the psalm (73:2–16) which so eloquently climaxes in verse 16.

The psalm indicates that the fortunes of the wicked will find reversals (73:18–20, 27). The "I" statements in this part of Psalm 73 confess the break in the relationship; however, the psalmist blends this confession of the polite and anti-social behavior of the psalmist to the unrelenting tenacity of God for the psalmist. The tenacity of God enables the faithfulness of the psalmist recounted in the statement of desire for God (73:25b).

> *When my mind turned itself bitter,*
> *When in my heart I was pricked,*
> *I was stupid and ignorant.*
> *I was like beasts toward you.*
> *But I was continually with you.*
> *And you hold my right hand.*
> *Whom do I have in heaven?*
> *And there is nothing on earth that I desire but you.* (73:21–23, 25)

This group of "I" statements prepares the reader for the final "I" statement. Here we find performative speech which, like the individual laments, expresses trust and connection between God and the believer. *I have made the Lord God my refuge* (73:28b).

Psalm 83, the other bookend of the Asaph psalms, does not exhibit the first person voice. Like other laments, it begins with a plea for the presence and voice of God. *O God, do not keep silent; do not hold your peace or be still, God* (83:2; Eng 1). The psalmist begins the Asaph booklet by looking for the resolution of anguished cognitive dissonance which is not elaborated in Psalm 83. There is a clear plea, however, for punishment on the enemies of God who happen to be the enemies of the psalmist also. For the editor of the Asaph collection God is the beginning of understanding but also the source of justice.

Psalm 75

The disclosure from God comes within a psalm of thanksgiving. The antiphonal texture of the psalm is evidenced as the writer goes through changes of voices: first person plural (75:2; Eng 1); first person divine (75:3–6; Eng 2–5); third person divine (75:7–9; Eng 6–8); first person believer (75:10; Eng 9); and finally first person divine (75:11; Eng 10).

The performative language is first person plural. *We give thanks to you. O God, we give thanks. And near is your name. They recount your wonderful deeds (75:2; Eng 1).* On the one hand, the performative speech introduces the next section of "I" statements of the psalm (75:3–6; Eng 2–5). On the other hand, the rationale for the performative language comes in the material that follows. The *kî* clause is the signal. The thanksgiving stands on two legs: the divine promise couched in "I" statements; and divine nature couched in third person confession language.

The "I" statements also reflect two movements. A promise begins the section using the language of stability. *When I set the time, I will judge with equity. When the earth totters and all its inhabitants, it is I who keep steady its pillars (75:3–4; Eng 2–3).* The second movement includes God's warning to the adversaries who the psalmist designates as the boastful and the wicked. However, the instruction to the adversaries strikes the cynical ear of the hearer. How can the boastful not boast and the wicked not raise their horn which is a symbol of power and, in this case, a symbol of arrogance?

The language of the psalm makes plain the conflict between the psalmist and the adversaries. Hence the psalmist moves on to a confession, not a first person confession such as the "I" statements of the laments, rather, a confession that describes the nature of God.

The psalmist begins with a crescendo using the negative sources. *For not from the east or from the west and not from the wilderness . . . for on the contrary God judges, God puts down this one and raises that one* (75:7–8; Eng 6–7).

We should notice the language of social conflict. The psalmist uses the image of up and down as a metaphor for social status. God warns the adversaries about their "uppitiness." God's action includes raising and lowering as symbols of social status and social conflict.

This same social conflict expresses that image of wine in the last part of the confession (75:9; Eng 8). The adversaries deserve the cup of God's wrath. The "cup of wrath" image occurs elsewhere in the Psalter (Ps 11:6) and in the prophetic tradition (see Isa 51:17,22; Jer 25:15; 49:12; Ezek 23:31–33; Hab 2:15–16; Zech 12:2). The same metaphor is picked up in the New Testament (Rev 14:10; 16:19; 17:4; 18:6). The psalmist seems to blend the "cup of wrath" tradition with the "trial by ordeal" image associated with poison, such as in Numbers 5:11–31. The Numbers text recounts a hypothetical case of a woman suspected of adultery who is given a potion which detects adultery in women. When the psalmist uses the image of drinking the cup of wrath, the psalmist assumes that those who *are* guilty shall surely *appear* guilty, as the woman in Numbers 5 did.[30] They receive full compensation for their sin by drinking the very last drop of the poison.

The psalmist, after the promise and the curse of the confession, returns to performative language in the first person. *I will witness forever and sing praises to the God of Jacob* (75:10; Eng 9).

God has the last word. The psalmist returns us to the first person divine. This language serves to connect this verse to the warning in the earlier verses exhorting the boastful and the wicked to eschew their haughtiness (75:5–6; Eng 4–5). Now the horns that they were not to raise are brought down by God (75:11; Eng 10).

This psalm does not include any memory language per se; however, it describes the contours of the historical aspect of the contextual self, namely the artifacts of faithful memory. The first artifact assumed by the psalmist was the name of God and the second was a promise that the social order will be turned around.

Psalm 78

Martin Buber argues that, in a historical age, the only way we know to talk about miracles is as an "abiding astonishment," something that continues to make us surprised and astonished in its presence. History itself, through God, generates an abiding astonishment.[31] The cultic prophet addresses this abiding astonishment even amidst the trauma of displacement.

Psalm 78 does not refer to the term *zākar* ("remember"). Instead it provides a recital of the history of God's salvation for the congregation. It gives the community the artifacts of re-memory, where other psalms provide exhortations to re-memory.

Psalm 81

When Hansel and Gretel went into the woods they thought that the crumbs they left would provide for an easy return home, but a bird ate the crumbs, and they were lost. We find ourselves in a situation like Hansel and Gretel's. The crumbs of memory that provide the way to our spiritual home have been eaten by the vulture of evil, contemporary preoccupation with the "now." But there is a way home. When the crumbs are gone the only way to get home is to remember home.

The psalmist shares with us a picture of God's "tough love." We see in this conversation an "I-Thou" dialogue.[32] In Psalm 81 we find the theme of God's unrelenting love. Once again the "I" we discover is a divine "I." Prophetic Yahweh speech comes through loud and clear (81:6b; Eng 5b). Through God's recital of memory maybe we can remember the way home. The general tone of the psalm reverberates with oracles against the nation. The psalmist has fused the oracle against the nation and the lament/plea form. This prophetic psalm echoes Psalms 50 and 95.[33] The remembering we find mentioned here is God's remembering.

The psalm begins with a festival shout (81:2–4; Eng 1–3) which appears to have been part of the Feast of Tabernacles.[34] Arguably, the Feast of Tabernacles, in Hebrew *sūkkōt* (Deut 16:13, 16; Lev 23:34), stood as the most important festival. It began as a farmers' feast, a celebration of ingathering and harvest, and eventually became a pilgrimage festival. People flowed into Jerusalem and into the central sanctuary. Ultimately, like the other major festivals of Passover and the Feast of Weeks, the Festival of Tabernacles connects with salvation history. The original farmers' festival becomes a time when the community remembered the huts during the wilderness time and the Exodus.[35] It was a time of memory.

The second section contains a Yahweh speech (81:6–17; Eng 5–16) in which God speaks in the first person using a prophet as a mouthpiece. God reveals salvation history beginning with the Exodus. God relieved the burden and freed our hands from the carrier's basket, both images of the slave's experience in Egypt.[36] We find a pattern of remembrance in the Yahweh speeches as we are reminded about the deliverance from Egypt and the gift of the Law. Yahweh raises a complaint with us regarding our response to this faithfulness.[37] We can discern the "I-Thou" tone in verse 8 (Eng 7). *In distress you called out, and I delivered you* (81:8a; Eng 7a). The speech continues to recount the salvation history.

Next we find a warning and a call to hear. *Listen/hear my people* (81:9a; Eng 8a). This warning tells us the danger that is about to befall us. The danger, idolatry, circles us like the crow that ate the crumbs of Hansel and Gretel, and we find ourselves reminded of the choruses of Deuteronomy (calls to hear, Deut 4:1; 5:1; 6:4; 9:1). The style of this cultic prophet resembles the Levitical preaching of Deuteronomy and Chronicles.[38]

There will be for you no strange/illicit god among you, and you will not do obeisance to a foreign god (81:10; Eng 9) seems to paraphrase the first commandment. *No strange gods will be for you before me* (Deut 5:7). Is this the crow that eats our crumbs, the crow of the idolatrous, illicit, and strange gods that have become so familiar?

The climax of the psalm comes in verse 11 (Eng 10). *I am the LORD your God who brought you up from the land of Egypt.* The psalmist has reversed the order of the Deuteronomic rendition of the Decalogue.

The admonition gives way to an imperative which anticipates the conclusion of the psalm. *Open your mouth wide, and I will fill it.* (81:11b; Eng 10b) However, before resolution, we must hear the lament of God that reminds us of God's pathos described in Hosea 11. *But my people did not listen to my voice* (81:12a; Eng 11a). God called and found the line was "busy." God looked and discovered that a crow had eaten our crumbs and that we could not find our way home.

The "tough love" of God left the world to its natural consequences, but that is not the end of the story. The last verse states *And God will feed them with the finest wheat, and from the rock with honey I (God) will satisfy you.*(81:17; Eng 16) God can provide sweet satisfaction where common sense tells us there are only rocks. As God rehearses history, we might find our history, our way.

How does the story of Hansel and Gretel end anyway? Do you think we can find our way home now? Can we eat that sweet honey in the rock? Re-memory reminds us that God's sustaining of the congregation does not cut us off from the present rather gives a historical perspective from which we anticipate the new inbreaking of the reign of God.

Summary: The Distinctive Asaphite Voice

The psalms of the Asaphites give a witness to cultic prophets. Sometimes they give witness to northern traditions reworked for the exilic and post-exilic context of faith. In fact, the booklet begins with Psalm 73 which speaks so eloquently about the temptations of the trauma of exile.

The recurring theme in the booklet involves the historical aspect of the contextual self, whether it is the language of memory (*zākar*) (Pss 74 and 77) or the recital of history (Ps 78). In this regard, we see that the cultic prophets remind us that we remain a historical people.

A disquieting element in reading the laments is the theme of the elusive presence of God, possibly even the absence of God. We cannot take the psalmist or the biblical texts seriously without being willing to entertain the idea that we sometime encounter God as silent.

LISTENING IN TO THE EARLY CHURCH

The task of memory returns the Christian community, time and time again, to the cross and resurrection. How do Christians dare exercise re-memory? Paul replies: *If we live, we live to the Lord, and if we die, we die to the Lord; so if we live or if we die, we are the Lord's.* (Rom 14:8–9) This is how Christians dare to practice re-memory. It doesn't matter if the memories are of the good or of the evil we have seen or experienced; we are the Lord's. Christians can struggle with re-memory only in Christ.

The theme of "remembrance" occurs also in the gospels in the story of the woman who washed Jesus' feet with her tears (Matt 26:6–13). *Truly I say to you, wherever this gospel is preached in the whole world, what she has done will be told in remembrance of her.*(Matt 26:13) Christianity understands the task of re-memory in the context of participation in the crucified and resurrected Christ. This story reminds us that Christianity locates re-memory in service as well.

We see the theme of remembrance as an organizing principle of the movement to write the gospels so that we might remember. Two expressions of this theme come through in the New Testament which the church has broken into two types of Christology, *christus victor* and *imitatio christi*. We remember the cross (*imitatio christi*) and the empty tomb (*christus victor*). These elements provide a common thread in each of the canonical gospels.

The priest uses the liturgy and communion in order to organize our memory. As such, *we remember the future.* The Lord's Supper anticipates the Messianic banquet. The historical trauma of the destruction of Jerusalem provided the crucible for the historical aspect of the contextual self of the Psalter; the scandal of the cross forges the historical and eschatological aspects of the contextual self today.

The Christian church celebrates memory in the Lord's Supper. In this process, the church remembers the future and dares the dangerous act of re-memory.

We remember the woman who washed Jesus' feet and do things in memory of her. We remember the *christus victor* and *imitatio christi*. All of these give us the triangle for eschatological existence as a historical aspect of the contextual self. These issues continue in the contemporary fiction of people of color.

Memory and Black Hymnody

Black hymnody has always contained a long narrative tradition. In the days in Africa, narrative song was commonplace. Narrative songs such as "Go Down Moses," "Joshua Fit the Battle of Jericho," and others were a staple in the liturgical diet of the slave church. The circumstance of Israel presented an analogy so that the slaves could sing:

> Little David was a shepherd boy,
> He killed Goliath and shouted for joy.

The problem of memory generates a cognitive dissonance when we perceive the prosperity of the wicked (Ps 73). Songs such as these echo Psalm 78 which recounts God's acts of salvation. Black hymnody generally remembers into the future, anticipating the coming prosperity.

However, two notable exceptions, "Were You There?" and "He Nevuh Said a Mumbalin' Word" outline the suffering Christ. Other "sorrow songs," like the Asaphite psalms, have a dimension of praise.[39] Like Psalm 80, which recounts the loss of favor, these songs build an empathy.

For Japanese Americans and the African Americans, reflection on certain events prompts re-memory. How can Japanese Americans practice re-memory when they see the prosperity Euro-American entrepreneurs gathered at the expense of interned Japanese Americans during World War II? How can the children of slave owners still prosper in the midst of the poverty of children of former slaves? These examples are similar and different at the same time. The ability of the U.S. to forget about the Japanese American internment outstrips the ability of the U.S. to forget about slavery. Slavery is a shared memory of Euro-American and African Americans requiring active forgetfulness. The internment of Japanese Americans, likewise, is a shared memory but localized in a way that has contributed to the way in which we avoid re-memory.

For some communities, re-memory is the process of history. Mexican Americans face discrimination in a land that once belonged to Mexico. The problem about memory is the dissonance it causes.

We have a history with the wicked. Both the heirs of the wicked and the heirs of the trauma share a common commitment to try not to practice re-memory. Our history with the wicked is one we try not to acknowledge.

Memory and Literature

As is the case with the Asaphite and Korahite psalms, we see the place of religious functionaries in contemporary literature. Toni Morrison draws a picture of two different types of religious functionaries. In her novel *Beloved,* Morrison lets us look at Baby Suggs, the life-giving preacher. She preaches in an open space, "the Clearing." She reminds Sethe that "it's time to lay it all down. . . . Lay all that mess down." [40] She reminds us that "in this place, we flesh; . . . love it . . . for this is the prize."[41] The memory of Baby Suggs is not historical like the psalms or the black hymnody we have discussed; rather it is the ontological re-memory of the trauma of slavery.

But Morrison also depicts a death-dealing preacher, who unlike Baby Suggs, has lost his way. Elias Whitcomb of Morrison's novel *The Bluest Eye* acts as an accomplice in the self-murder of a black girl who wished her eyes were blue. When the little black girl, Pecola, went to him for religious advice, he suggested that she pray for blue eyes. He said she would receive them if she prayed earnestly; he assured her of that.[42]

Religious tradition has many forms. The Mexican American literature of Rudolfo Anaya and others has retained a sense of the religion of the indigenous peoples of North America and orthodox Christianity. Both the priest and the *curandera* provide the voice of the religious functionary in the novel *Bless me, Ultima.* The priest draws the young Antonio to a religion that rejects the history of the indigenous religion. On the other hand, the *curandera*, Ultima, keeps him close to those religious roots.

The challenge of memory and culture comes through in Richard Rodriguez's *Hunger for Memory*: "I could not forget that schooling was changing me and separating me from the life I enjoyed before becoming a student."[43] In contemporary culture, education and religion shape the self. So his comments about education in the world of the dominant culture mirrors a theological world that grew out of the education of the dominant culture. "In contrast to the Catholicism of School, the Mexican Catholicism of home was less concerned with man the sinner than with man the supplicant."[44]

Ultima leads Antonio through this maze in Anaya's novel, but the education of Richard Rodriguez makes it more difficult for him to touch the indigenous elements of his culture and faith. The memory here is not historical, in the narrow sense of the word, but historical in the sociological sense. The contextual self is located in a specific history. When that umbilical cord is cut, no one else's historical aspect of the contextual self can provide life-giving nutrients.

Religious functionaries manage the task of re-memory for the community, but re-memory is a task that falls to everyone. Toni Morrison acts as the midwife who births the re-memory of slavery. She structures her novel *Beloved* to mimic the human memory. People remember a bit at a time. Thus, the story does not unfold in a linear way, but in a combination of recurring flashes.

Her topic was a haunted house and self-murder, and her vehicle for the reflection was re-memory. She began with the story of Margaret Garner, a black woman and mother who ran away from slavery in the South. When the slave catchers came to take her and her children back, she went to an old shed behind the house where she killed one child and attempted to kill two others, maiming them for life. She was about to kill the last child when she was stopped.

However, in order to excavate this story fully, Morrison had to remember slavery. She spoke as an African American when she said, "We do not remember. For if we remembered, how could we get up and go to work every day?" Likewise for the nation, slavery eats away at the moral fiber of a nation committed to freedom. Hence, not remembering becomes a survival tactic. Because of our penchant for forgetting, remembering often requires research and intentionality.

The contextual self demands re-memory, not for the broader theological purpose, but for everyday use and life. Alice Walker recounts the story of three women, Maggie, Dee, and their mother. Maggie, the shy one, burned herself trying to save the house during a fire. Dee got the college education and the good looks. Their mother provided strength and sustenance for the family. Dee comes back for a short visit.

Now Dee has changed her name. She finds the furniture in the old house quaint. She asks her mother for two old quilts which had been made by Maggie's grandmother and other relatives. These quilts however, have been promised to Maggie as a wedding gift. But Dee knows they are priceless quilts, and she wants to hang them prominently in her home. She knows Maggie will simply keep them for everyday use.[45]

This story gives us a parable about memory and heritage. The aim of memory is everyday use, a vehicle to deal with the crises of everyday life.

The contextual self maintains that there is a place that gives witness to the reign of God, a place that causes us to critique every expression of power and place in light of the displacement. It's not that we have experienced Zion, but rather the displacement the awareness of Zion engenders.

The contextual self proposes that the reign of God provides the context for the memory of God's delivering and our trauma. How can we dare to practice re-memory? The "how" is in Christ. The context is everyday use; for when we do not remember, we rebel and lose our way.

In a culture of disbelief, such as ours, one might construe the task of uncovering the anthropology of the Psalter simply in terms of excavating the anthropology of a specific community, living in a particular place and time, that happened to have certain religious notions. This book, on the contrary, proclaims that the understandings of the self one encounters in the Psalter reveal a *theological* anthropology, one in which the doctrine of God is essential to the task of understanding what humanity is. When one finds the self of the Psalter, one discovers a community whose self sprouts from the theological affirmation of the reign of God. In this regard it comprises a self rooted in God's self-assertion as the beginning of the self of the Psalter.

The reign of God gives logic to the pleas of the conflictual self. The conflictual self expresses an awareness of God's self-assertion in the past that does not seem to have a counterpart in the present. As such, these psalms recount the theme of the absence of God. In other words, there would be no reason to lament a God who is not sovereign. The personal piety of the Psalter gives witness to the reign of God.

The self-assertion of God constitutes the bones, muscles, and sinew of the *YHWH mlk* psalms. These psalms outline the reign of God beyond the conventional limits of neighborhood. God's self-assertion empowers the authoritative self. This authoritative self demands serious attention to the role of human moral agency by believers. The official religion draws the picture of the authoritative self.

The official religion also notes the self-assertion of God in the story of God's people and their location. The story is history and memory. The location, Zion, functions not as nostalgia but rather as a critique of the present place, just as history and memory function as the critique of the present exercise of power. For both history and place fall short of the reign of God that remains the measuring stick for the self of the Psalter.

Through this search for the self in the Psalter one also uncovers a cross-cultural dialogue. The colored church finds identity in the God whose self-assertion the Psalter time and again proclaims. This book claims that past attempts to understand theological anthropology suffer from a crippling ethnocentrism. Such a style of reflection on theological anthropology, whether the resource is biblical or philosophical theology, can afford neither a naive nor a self-consciously imperialistic ethnocentrism. Rather, if we are to learn what it means to be human, we must do it through listening in to the Scriptures and each other's cultures.

NOTES

Chapter 1

1. Robert Reich, *Tales of a New America* (New York: Times Books, 1987), 53-55.
2. Klaus Westermann, *Praise and Lament* (Atlanta: John Knox, 1981), 185.
3. Walter Brueggemann, "The Costly Loss of Lament," *JSOT* 36 (1986): 59.
4. O. Keel, *The Symbolism of the Biblical World: Ancient Near Eastern Iconography and the Book of Psalms* (New York: Seabury, 1978), 78.
5. Harry Birkeland in his books *Die Feinde des Individuum* (Oslo: Gröndahl, 1933) and *The Evildoers in the Book of Psalms* (Oslo: Jacob Dybwald, 1955) argues that generally the enemies are Gentiles. Stanley Rosenbaum ("The Concept of the 'Antagonist' in Hebrew Psalm Poetry" (Ph.D. dissertation, Brandeis University, 1974) proposes that we find two different words for enemies and they have different semantic ranges.
6. Steven J. L. Croft, *The Identity of the Individual*, (Sheffield: Sheffield Academic Press, 1987), 135.
7. Craig Broyles, "The Conflict of Faith and Experience in the Psalms: A Form-Critical and Theological Study," *JSOTSS* 52 (Sheffield: JSOT Press, 1989), 184.
8. Walter Brueggemann, *The Message of the Psalms: A Theological Commentary*, Augsburg Old Testament Series (Minneapolis: Augsburg, 1984), 126.
9. See *Songs of Zion: African-American Hymn Book for the Methodist Church* (Nashville: Abingdon, 1981), 183.
10. Peter Craigie, *Psalms 1-50*, Word Biblical Commentary 19 (Waco: Word, 1983), 224.
11. Richard Wright, *Native Son* (New York: HarperCollins, 1993).
12. Croft, *The Identity of the Individual*, 141.
13. Marvin E. Tate, *Psalms 51-100* (Waco: Word, 1983), 135.
14. Susan Sontag, *Illness as Metaphor* (New York: Vintage, 1979).
15. Fabry, "Dal" *TDOT III*, 219.
16. Croft, *The Identity of the Individual*, 149.
17. Reinhold Niebuhr, *Moral Man and Immoral Society: A Study in Ethics and Politics* (New York: Scribners, 1932), xiii.
18. For an excellent discussion of how this relates to matters of race, see Cornel West, *Keeping Faith: Philosophy and Race in America* (New York: Routledge, 1993), 252-53.
19. Anaya, *Bless Me, Ultima* (Berkeley: Quinto Sol, 1972), 4.
20. Dwight Hopkins and George Cummings, *Cut Loose Your Stammering Tongue* (Maryknoll: Orbis, 1992), 38.
21. Toni Morrison, *Beloved* (New York: Knopf, 1987), 89.
22. Ibid., 3, 169, 239.
23. Ibid., 32-35.
24. Sandra Cisneros, *The House on Mango Street* (New York: Vintage, 1989), 59.
25. Morrison, *Beloved*, 148.

26. Elie Wiesel, *Night* (New York: Bantam, 1960), 62.

Chapter 2

1. Reich, *Tales of a New America*, 201.
2. Ibid., 201.
3 Sigmund Mowinckel, *The Psalms in Israel's Worship* (New York: Abingdon, 1962), 1:107.
4. Like Marvin Tate in his excellent commentary, I eschew the use of the loaded term "enthronement psalms." Marvin Tate, *Psalms 51–100*, Word Biblical Commentary 20 (Dallas: Word, 1990), 505.
5. John Watts, "*Yahweh Malak* Psalms," *ThLZ* 21 (1965), 343.
6. Mowinckel, *The Psalms in Israel's Worship*, 1:108.
7. Ibid., 1:111.
8. Ibid., 1:112.
9. Ibid., 1:113.
10. Ibid., 1:117.
11. Hans-Joachim Kraus, *Psalms 60–150* (Minneapolis: Augsburg, 1989).
12. Tate, *Psalms 51–100*, 507.
13. Ben C. Ollenburger, *Zion, The City of the Great King: A Theological Symbol of the Jerusalem Cult*, JSOTSS 41 (Sheffield: JSOT Press, 1987), 27f.
14. Tate, *Psalms 51–100*, 531–32.
15. Mowinckel, *The Psalms in Israel's Worship*, 1:106.
16. Hithpael.
17. Carroll Stuhlmueller, *Psalms 2: A Biblical-Theological Commentary*," OTM 22 (Wilmington: Michael Glazier, 1983), 87.
18. Bernhard Anderson, *Out of the Depths* (Philadelphia: Westminster, 1988), 140.
19. Kraus, *Psalms 60–150*, 32.
20. Robert Reich, *The Work of Nations: Preparing Ourselves for the Twenty-first Century Capitalism* (New York: Knopf, 1991), 268–81.
21. Gerald H. Wilson, *The Editing of the Hebrew Psalter*, SBLDS 76 (Atlanta: Scholars, 1985), 215.
22. Gerhard E. Lenski, *Power and Privilege: A Theory of Social Stratification* (Chapel Hill: University of North Carolina Press, 1984), 168–76.
23. Keith W. Whitelam, *The Just King: Monarchical Judicial Authority*, JSOTSS 12 (Sheffield: JSOT Press, 1979), 29.
24. Tryggve Mettinger, *King and Messiah: The Civil and Sacral Legitimation of the Israelite Kings* (Lund: CWK Gleerup, 1976), 101.
25. Ian Engnell, *Studies in Divine Kingship in the Ancient Near East* (Oxford: Blackwell, 1967) 174–77.
26. J.H. Eaton, *Kingship and the Psalms* (Naperville: Allenson, 1976), 117.
27. Psalm 18 parallels 2 Samuel 22, but we will not have space to explore the points of contact in this context.
28. James Luther Mays, *Psalms*, Interpretation: A Bible Commentary for Teaching and Preaching (Louisville: Westminster/John Knox Press, 1994), 90.
29. Peter C. Craigie, *Psalms 1–50*, Word Biblical Commentary 19 (Waco: Word, 1983), 167, 170. The Hebrew of the MT is difficult here. See Craigie for a full discussion of the problems.

30. Eaton, *Kingship and the Psalms,* 120.
31. Kraus, *Psalms 60–150,* 77.
32. Carroll Stuhlmueller, *Psalms 1,* OTM 21 (Wilmington: Michael Glazier, 1983), 319.
33. Tate, *Psalms 51–100,* 223-24
34. Ibid., 225.
35. Ibid.
36. Ibid., 409. See also with reference to "my son" Kraus, *Psalms 60–150,* 204.
37. Gösta W. Ahlström, *Psalm 89: Eine Liturgie aus dem Ritual des leiden Königs* (Lund: CWK Gleerups, 1959).
38. Mettinger, *King and Messiah,* 254.
39. Here the writing of Rita Nakashima Brock is most interesting; see her "Ending Innocence and Nurturing Willfulness," in Carol Adams and Marie Fortune, eds., *Violence Against Women and Children: A Christian Theological Sourcebook* (New York: Continuum, 1995), 71–84.
40. Mettinger, *King and Messiah.* 257–58.
41. Eaton, *Kingship and the Psalms,* 124.
42. Ibid.
43. Mettinger, *King and Messiah,* 104.
44. Ibid., 260.

Chapter 3

1. Mowinckel, *The Psalms in Israel's Worship,* 2:53-73. For a more recent treatment see Harry P. Nasuti, *Tradition History and the Psalms of Asaph,* SBLDS 88 (Atlanta: Scholars, 1988), 127-29.
2. Larry E. Thompson, "Jean Toomer: As Modern Man" in Arna Bontemps, ed., *The Harlem Renaissance Remembered* (New York: Dodd, Mead, 1972), 51-62; Barbara Bowen, "Untroubled Voice: Call and Response in *Cane*" in Henry Louis Gates, Jr., ed., *Black Literature & Literary Theory* (New York: Methuen, 1984), 187-203.
3. Sandra Cisneros, *The House on Mango Street* (New York: Vintage, 1989), 3.
4. Ibid.
5. C. Stuhlmueller, *Psalms 1,* 242.
6. Craigie, *Psalms 1-50,* 343.
7. Ibid., 344.
8. Stuhlmueller, *Psalms 1,* 241.
9. Ollenburger, *Zion,* 41.
10. Ibid., 74.
11. Stuhlmueller, *Psalms 1,* 243.
12. Hans-Joachim Kraus, *Psalms 1-59* (Minneapolis: Augsburg, 1988), 463.
13. Craigie, *Psalms 1-50,* 345.
14. Ollenburger, *Zion,* 77.
15. J. Clinton McCann, *A Theological Introduction to the Psalms: The Psalms as Torah* (Nashville: Abingdon, 1993), 151.
16. A teenage boy sang in the junior choir in his small Baptist church; but every week he would fall asleep during the sermon. One Sunday after church his mother took him to the side and said, "Stevie, it is all right for you to sleep during the sermon, but you cannot snore." Her point was that the place generated certain manners, church manners if you will.

17. Ollenburger, *Zion*, 145-62.

18. Jürgen Roloff, *The Revelation of John: A Continental Commentary* (Minneapolis: Augsburg, 1993), 91.

19. R. H. Charles notes the prophetic connections but misses the Psalms connection. See Charles, "The Revelation to St. John," *ICC* (New York: Charles Scribner's Sons, 1920), 1:183.

20. Roland de Vaux, *Ancient Israel: Religious Institutions* (New York: McGraw-Hill, 1961), 2:392.

21. Martin Buss, "The Psalms of Asaph and Korah," *JBL* 82 (1962): 387.

22. Harry Peter Nasuti, *Tradition History and the Psalms of Asaph* (Atlanta: Scholars, 1988), 187.

23. Ibid., 188.

24. Ibid., 187.

25. Brevard Childs, *Memory and Tradition in Israel*, SBT 37 (London: SCM Press, 1962), 74.

26. Nasuti, *Tradition History*, 117-29.

27. Anne Wilson Schaef, *When Society Becomes an Addict* (San Francisco: Harper, 1987), 70-71.

28. McCann, *A Theological Introduction to the Book of Psalms*, 143; See also Walter Brueggemann, "Bounded By Obedience and Praise," *JSOT* 50 (1986): 81.

29. Perdue outlines the argument for the wisdom provenance of this psalm. See Leo Perdue, *Wisdom and Cult*, SBLDS 30 (Missoula: Scholars, 1977), 287.

30. Tate, *Psalms 51-100*, 259.

31. Walter Brueggemann, *Abiding Astonishment: Psalms, Modernity, and the Making of History*, Literary Currents in Biblical Interpretation (Louisville: Westminster/John Knox, 1991), 31.

32. Stuhlmueller, *Psalms 2*, 40.

33. Kraus, *Psalms 60-150*, 147.

34. Ibid., 148.

35. deVaux, *Ancient Israel*, 495-502.

36. Kraus, *Psalms 60-150*, 151.

37. Thijs Booij, "The Background of the Oracle in Psalm 81," *Bib* 65 (1984): 465-75.

38. Tate, *Psalms 51-100*, 321.

39. Jon M. Spencer, *Black Hymnody: A Hymnological History of the African American Church* (Knoxville: University of Tennessee, 1992), 68-69.

40. Morrison, *Beloved*, 86.

41. Ibid., 88-89.

42. Toni Morrison, *The Bluest Eye* (New York: Washington Square, 1970), 130-44.

43. Richard Rodriguez, *Hunger for Memory: The Education of Richard Rodriguez* (New York: Bantam, 1982), 45.

44. Ibid., 85.

45. Alice Walker, "Everyday Use," *In Love and Trouble* (New York: Harvest, 1973), 47-59.